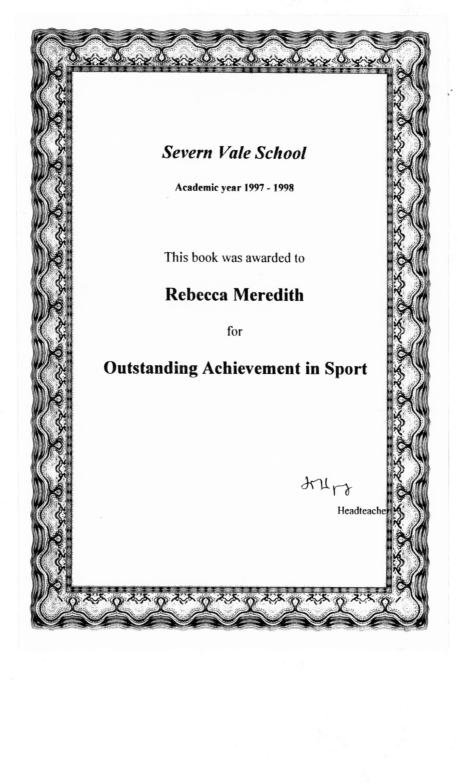

Severn Vale School

Academic year 1997 - 1998

This book was awarded to

Rebecca Meredith

for

Outstanding Achievement in Sport

Headteacher

What the reviewers are saying about the

Chairlift Ski Guide

"*All-Terrain Skiing* will revolutionize instructional ski books. In fact, calling this an instructional book seems the wrong label. Maybe the Skiing Scriptures will do. Or perhaps the Tao of Downhill."

Mike Finkel
Skiing Magazine

"The Extreme Team Advanced Ski Clinics have been a sell-out event for seven years. Our guests rave about the drills and techniques taught by Dan Egan."

Susie Barnett-Burshong
Grand Targhee Ski Resort

"Mihaela Fera-Egan provides great motivation. Her personality plus her racing accomplishments equal a coach with a personal touch perfect for adults and children."

Gus Demaggio, Head Coach
Loon Mountain Race Team

"I've taken clinics with Dan and Mihaela throughout North America and New Zealand. Thanks to them, I finally broke out of my skiing rut."

Eric Foch, Mortgage Broker
New York, NY

This book is designed to accompany the "Chairlift Ski Guide" video, which demonstrates the 38 drills in the book.

To order the "Chairlift Ski Guide" video, call 1.800.619.6801. Retail Cost: $29.95.

Mention your favorite drill in the book and save $5.00 when you order the "Chairlift Ski Guide" video.

You'll pay only $24.95.

All-Terrain Skiing

Dan Egan

The Egan Entertainment Network

A Joshua Tree Press Book

Published by
World Leisure Corporation
Hampstead, New Hampshire

World Leisure Corporation, P.O. Box 160, Hampstead, NH 03841

Copyright © 1996 by Dan Egan and Jack B. Rochester

A Joshua Tree Press Book
Cherry Hill Farm, Cherry Hill Road, Grafton, NH 03240
tel: 603.523.8350; fax: 603.523.8343

Distributed to the trade in U.S.A. by
LPC Group, Login Trade, 1436 West Randolph Street,
Chicago, IL 60607
tel: 312.733.8228; 800.626.4330

Distributed to the trade in Canada by
E.A. Milley Enterprises, Inc., Locust Hill, Ontario L0H 1J0
tel: 800.399.6858
Distributed to the trade in U.K. by
Roger Lascelles, 47 York Road, Brentford, Middlesex TW8 0QP
tel: 0181.847.0935

Mail Order, Ski Shop, and Catalog sales by
Egan Entertainment Network
P.O. Box 1305, Lincoln, NH 03251
tel: 800.619.6801

U.S. Military and Special Sales by
World Leisure Corporation, 177 Paris Street, Boston, MA 02128
tel: 617.569.1966; fax: 617.561.7654
e-mail: wleisure@aol.com

ISBN: 0-915009-53-6

Dedication

Dedicated to all who wonder about the impossible.

What is your vision for your world?

How do you see yourself performing
within your vision?

Do you believe in the unbelievable?

ALL-TERRAIN SKIING

ALL-TERRAIN SKIING

TABLE OF CONTENTS

Time Out   67

Fluidity Section   69

Agility Section   87

All-Terrain Ski Stories   105

Training   126

Foreword

In my 25 years as a skier and nearly a decade as an editor of *Skiing* magazine, I have worked out a highly specialized system of classifying top-notch skiers. There are expert skiers, extreme skiers, ski bums, ski stars, ski instructors, ski pros — and then there is Dan Egan.

Dan is the most dedicated, most spirited, most head-over-heels-in-love-with-sliding-on-snow skier I have ever encountered. He eats skiing; he breathes skiing; hell, he sweats skiing. He has traveled the world preaching the gospel of skiing — a one-man mogul-skiing missionary — the Johnny Appleseed of face-shots. His movies, which always bring to life the cultures and ski scenes of unimaginable lands, are the skiing equivalent of a National Geographic special. I have never met anyone quite like him. Dan is so far beyond normal classifications of skiers that there was no choice but to grant him a category all to himself.

First introduced to Dan as a student in one of his clinics, at a small Vermont ski area called Bolton Valley, I was immediately struck by his unique insights, his effortless humor, and his endearing eccentricity. His energy is unparalleled: a ski lesson with Dan is part Einstein, part Freud, and part Groucho Marx. A full-soul approach to skiing, I call it. A dozen of his personalized pointers — one about edging on ice, another about absorbing moguls, a third about maintaining a quiet upper body — and several of his bad jokes remain with me, to recall when I'm having an off-day on the slopes.

I have skied with him several times since, and his unflagging enthusiasm has never failed to fill me with joy. I have always had the impression that life, for Dan, is a perpetual powder day. To take a few runs with him is always a season highlight, no matter what the ski conditions are.

I've been waiting for years for Dan to write a book like this, so that his unusual ideas are readily accessible to all skiers. In quintessential Dan — clear, concise, bizarre — *All-Terrain Skiing* will revolutionize the instructional ski book. In fact, calling this an instructional book seems the wrong label. Maybe the Skiing Scriptures will do. Or perhaps the Tao of Downhill. Only a book cooked up by Dan could have drills called BE A BIRD, MIND OVER MOGUL and FUNNY WALK TURN. Only a book by Dan would ask you to take your skis off and walk down the hill. Only Dan will ask you to flap your arms as you ski, or clap your hands, or ski with your boots unbuckled. There is material in here to help and amuse and enlighten every level of skier.

So stifle your inhibitions, drop your doubts, and open your mind. Read this book, study it, bring the cards on the chairlift. Ease into Dan's world. Laugh at the tales of his crazy adventures. And discover a whole new way to improve your skiing.

Mike Finkel
September 7, 1996
Bozeman, Montana

Acknowledgments

It is impossible to recall the countless chairlift conversations and ski days as a ski student, racer, professional athlete, coach, and ski enthusiast. Together with family members, friends, colleagues, acquaintances, and strangers, I have had the pleasure of searching for the ultimate turn again and again around the globe. I love the passionate discussions starting from the excitement of one day and ending with the anticipation of the next. To me, that is where the inner science and the soul of skiing exist off the mountain.

I wish to thank all six of my brothers and sisters, Mary Ellen, Bob, John, Sue, Ned, and Mike. Growing up in a skiing family on hand-me-down equipment, whether hiking up in our back yard to ski 200 feet down, at the local ski area, or on a Saturday trip to the mountains, we always had each other to ski with and we always had fun. A special thanks to my mother and father for having the patience and willingness to wake up and get us to the ski bus every Saturday, and especially for allowing me to choose my career in skiing. There is a little bit of both of them in this book.

My brother John and I have a special bond. Together we have climbed and skied worldwide. There will be more trips and fresh tracks, but I am grateful for the memories and knowledge learned so far, which have made me a better man.

With regard to specific ideas and concepts, I would like to thank the following people for their contributions: Susie Barnett-Burshong, Ed Brennan, Lizzy Day, Tom Day, Hank de'Vre, Dean Decas, Gus Demaggio, Eric and Rob DesLauriers, David Deutl, Mike Finkle, Eric Foch, Tom Grissom, Josh Lerman, Wade McKoy, Blake Miller, Warren Miller, Dennis Ouellette, Glenn Parkinson, Doug Pfeiffer, David Seymore, Allen St. John, Bernie Weichsel, and all the clients from the Extreme Team Advanced Ski Clinics.

In putting this book together, I owe a great big thank you to Jack Rochester and Joan Paterson of Joshua Tree Press. Without their help, my thoughts would still be in my head. Patrick Media Productions coordinated the production of the video. Jay Klebeck, Bill Patrick, Patrick Stork, Tim Horigan, and Frank Loftus all played a role in editing, shooting, and making good ideas better. My friends at Preseps Ltd. coordinated the packaging, design, and my countless corrections to the cards. To Ed Farrington, Dan Hale, Maureen Farrington, Matt Borlaug, Roger Gaides, David Cote, and Walter Flinn – thank you. Photographer Denis Welsh is a personal friend and a great photographer. Charlie Leocha and World Leisure Corporation kept me on track and provided the guidance to see the project through to the end. Video Action Sports and Jeff Reynolds have continued to distribute my films and support my efforts for over six years. Without them, few people would see my films.

My wife, Mihaela Fera-Egan, has been a constant positive force in my life. Her input, experience, and confidence are invaluable. This project is a result of our love for the sport of skiing and for each other.

Dan Egan
Lincoln, New Hampshire
September, 1996

Introduction

I was never too cool for ski school. Nevertheless, I was exposed to ski lessons from the time I was five until I was seventeen. Every winter Saturday, my brothers and sisters and I would jump on a bus and head north to ski country with the Blizzard Ski Club. The club had a patch system that indicated your ski school level. I set out to have every patch sewn on the arm of my ski jacket. By the time I was 14, I had graduated to the Demo Team, the highest level of achievement. We were the few and the proud.

Years later, during an interview with *Skiing* magazine, the writer asked me: "How did a kid from a suburb of Boston grow up to become one of the top extreme skiers in the world?" At that moment, I realized the importance of ski school. All those Saturday lessons and the basic ski techniques taught by competent ski instructors, combined with a powerful desire to become the best at whatever I set my mind to, made me the skier I am today.

In my *Chairlift Ski Guide* package, you'll learn 38 ski drills designed to make you a better skier. What you won't find is a lot of ski jargon and technical discussions of ski designs. My program is modeled on the intensive workshops I teach to skiers around the world. It demands that you practice it regularly and passionately. If you do, I promise that you will see results.

The foundation of my approach is based on body mechanics and the principles of Ecomotion. Ecomotion is the ecological relationship between your body and the earth. Ecomotion is economy of movement.

Ecomotion teaches you to take an intelligent and ecologically conservative approach to your physical conditioning and the use of your body in active sports, such as skiing. Using Ecomotion, you'll develop a new awareness of your relationship to gravity in varying ski conditions, how to dynamically orient and angulate your body to maximize your control and efficiency, and how to achieve the constant, fluid motion of the professional skier.

Skiing is not an intellectual activity; it is a simple physical activity based on good body position. Keep these four principles in mind and you'll soon be skiing better than ever:

- good balance
- powerful stance with shoulders square to the hill
- eyes focused up or down the hill
- proper hand position

The drills in my program will help you become aware of every aspect of your body positioning in order to improve your carving turns, bump skiing, and all-terrain ability. The drills are designed to take your mind off your skiing and focus your body energy on the task at hand. I have found that when we allow our bodies to react to a situation, overall athletic performance is enhanced. Skiers who take my workshops have proven it thousands of times over.

To receive the maximum benefit from your investment, use this program often – but please use it in the way it was designed. Note that there are five sections: Balance, Upper Body, Power, Fluidity, and Agility. Every skier should begin with Balance. Assess your skills and your skill level, then work on mastering one section or set of cards at a time. Each drill complements every other drill in the package, so skipping some and trying others out of order won't give you the maximum benefit. Perform each drill in order and master every aspect of it.

Congratulations on taking the first step to better skiing. While you're teaching your body this new way of skiing, please also remember to have fun!

How to Use this Package

"I have been skiing for years, read every book there is to read, seen all the how-to videos, and still haven't improved as a skier. What am I doing wrong?"

As a professional skier, racer, ski film producer, trainer, and educator, I've heard countless people ask me this question. Quite honestly, most of these recreational skiers aren't doing anything *wrong*. It's simply that most tools for learning are inadequate. They aren't far-reaching enough. They aren't interactive. Execution is critical in skiing and when you want to try out that new technique, you just can't take the lesson out on the slopes.

It's Difficult to Learn to Ski Better

Spending an evening in an easy chair reading a book on ski techniques may be a great idea. Watching an instructional ski video is fine, so far as it goes. The problem arises when you're out on the slopes the next day and it's time to remember what you read or viewed so that you can perform it. Unfortunately, most people simply don't have the presence of mind to do this.

Skiing is about performance, not practice. As Nike has drummed into us, you gotta *just do it*. Most skiers I've trained pick up technique quickly when they see it performed; that's because 80 percent of what we learn is visual. But there's a down side too: it's much harder to imitate an image we're trying to recollect in our mind than one we're watching right in front of us.

How, then, to learn or improve? The logical choice would be to take lessons at the ski slope. After all, every modern ski area offers ski schools. The sad truth is that most skiers cringe at the thought of ski lessons and would do anything to avoid the perceived embarrassment of learning better skiing techniques in front of others. Besides, skiing is fun – lessons aren't. For most Americans, slopeside ski school is considered something for children or beginners.

Most people believe they can learn to ski without formal instruction. Most would rather improve their skiing on their own. In fact, up to a certain point of performance ability, learning to ski is relatively easy. Most skiers can get down the groomed lower slopes of a family ski area, but what about skiers who want to challenge the peaks or the mogul fields? Short of specialized ski clinics like my brother John and I teach, there really isn't any way for them to improve. Now there is a way: the *Chairlift Ski Guide*.

Learning by Skiing: A Multimedia Approach

The *Chairlift Ski Guide* is a multimedia learning package for beginning and intermediate skiers. At the heart of my approach are the ten rules of safe skiing, which are woven throughout the program. The package consists of three learning tools:

- Dan Egan's *All-Terrain Skiing*, a paperback book, with complete lessons and instructions.

- "Chairlift Ski Guide" with Dan Egan, an instructional videotape, synchronized with the drills in the book and enlivened with entertaining, informative demonstrations by, and interviews with, experienced skiers.

- Dan Egan's Chairlift Ski Guide cards, a pocket-size set of instructional cards that teach and reinforce specific tips and techniques.

As a complete, self-instructional, multimedia learning package, the *Chairlift Ski Guide* teaches skiers everything they need to know about skiing. The program is divided into five categories: Balance, Upper Body, Power, Fluidity, and Agility, with a varying number of individual drills within each category. As you read, keep in mind that skiing involves the following elements:

Mind. Most skiers don't understand that they need to be mentally prepared as well as physically in shape to ski. I begin with an understanding of the human mind and body, exploring desire, confidence, and will power.

Body. I'm always amazed to see skiers arise, drink a cup of coffee, then head up the slopes and wonder why they have burning thighs by ten o'clock. Skiers learn stretching and warm-up routines here, as well as how to develop their movement techniques.

Equipment. There are proper ways to use ski equipment – skis, boots, poles – as well as clothing, and they are covered in this program.

Conditions. One thing is certain: the skier will always encounter changing terrain and conditions. This program teaches the skills needed for skiing everything from groomed trails to powder.

An Integrated Learn-to-Ski-Better Program

The *Chairlift Ski Guide* package is an integrated, self-contained program for beginning and intermediate skiers who want to ski better. The book and the video are organized for progressive learning. There are 38 drills and each takes approximately ten minutes to complete. Lessons in the book are synchronized with those on the video; however, the book provides depth and detail not found on the video, For its part, the video concentrates on maximizing the visual aspects of the drills and techniques explained more fully in the book. Using the book and video together results in highly productive learning and better time management – ten minutes per lesson – than any competing stand-alone book or video can provide.

At the heart of the *Chairlift Ski Guide* program is a set of 19 pocket-size, double-sided, laminated instructional cards for ready reference. You will find these cards inserted in this book, as near as possible to the drills they are designed to be used with. Remove the cards from the book and separate them for use. The cards are designed to be strung together on a lavaliere or slipped into a zippered pocket.

Each drill in the book and on the video is found on corresponding cards that provide, in color photos and text, a step-by-step guide for developing a particular skill or technique or for skiing particular types of snow conditions. *All three are designed to be used together.*

In addition, each lesson in all three elements of the *Chairlift Ski Guide* package is color- and shape-keyed, using the international skiing trail symbols. Thus, a Green Circle is beginner, a Blue Square is intermediate, and the Black Diamond is expert. The symbol appears in the top-right corner of the card, at the top of the first page of each drill in the book, and continuously in the video. Thus, Drill 3 in the Power section (Power Slide) appears as 9A — Blue Square. Drill 2 in the Agility section (Three-Step Turn) appears as 16B – Black Diamond.

The *Chairlift Ski Guide* is the most innovative way to improve skiing skills while out skiing on the slopes. Skiers of all ability levels will appreciate learning how to handle different conditions and situations as they actually encounter them.

Ideally, skiers take the *Chairlift Ski Guide* program with them for the ski weekend. Arriving at their accommodations, they read the book and watch the video, perhaps alternating between the two. The skier selects cards from the *Chairlift Ski Guide* to take to the slopes the next morning. Each card features the following:

- Title or subject in large boldface type at the top of the card

- Lesson identifier symbol and reference number in the top-right corner

- Short introduction and easy-to-follow drills and techniques in one to two sentences

- Step-by-step photos

- Simple, descriptive instructions adjacent to each photo

Now that you understand how the three tools in the *Chairlift Ski Guide* package are integrated, take a few minutes right now to use the three together. Then read the following essays to help you prepare for the slopes where you can work with the entire program.

All-Terrain Skiing

Relax, You're Skiing

I am going to reveal skiing's best-kept secret. The essence of skiing can be expressed in one word: *smile*. Skiing is not brain surgery; lose the compulsion to improve. Relax, you're skiing. Have fun and enjoy the mountains. Be happy out in the fresh mountain air, sliding over snow, and practice enjoying the mountain experience.

The best part about skiing is that you don't have to be good to enjoy it. Today's high-tech grooming machinery has increased the amount of skiable terrain. That makes skiing an enjoyable event for everyone. Skiing is a unique winter sport. The sensation of speed

Skiers steer with their feet, angulate with their knees and hips, absorb with their legs and arms.

mixed with gliding down the mountain, pulled by gravity, makes skiing a truly special experience. Next time you're out on the hill, take the focus off your ability and place it on your surroundings and, oddly enough, your ability just might get better.

Skiing is about constant fluid motion down the hill. The only way for our bodies to be in constant fluid motion is to be relaxed. Think about being calm and strong, limber and loose. Try not to be tense. When I get nervous on skis, I stop, take a couple of deep breaths and shake my body like a rag doll. This action reminds me to relax and ski loose. It also makes me laugh at myself, which helps me to enjoy this sport I love so much.

While skiing, our body parts need to be moving in different directions at the same moment. This calls for isolation of body parts. Break your body down into several groups: arms, shoulders, hips, knees, and feet. Skiers steer with their feet, angulate with their knees and hips, absorb with their legs and arms. They have silent shoulders and constantly readjust balance with hands and ski poles. There is a lot happening all at once and the key is to be fluid and smooth. The best way to make this happen is to be flexible, calm, and strong.

I always tell people that if you want to become a better skier, make sure that your last conscious act before you push off and head down the mountain is to smile. A smile sends good positive vibrations throughout the entire body. Researchers have proven that it is impossible to be tense and have a genuine smile at the same time. You may be surprised how often you forget to smile before you start down a trail. Train your mind to remember to smile. It is a very valuable tool and one you'll want to master in skiing. Use it — you'll be glad you did, and remember, "Relax, you're skiing."

Fuel Your Furnace

In 1978, Ingemar Stenmark was my hero. I was 14 years old and attending a Christmas Ski Racing Camp at Waterville Valley, New Hampshire. I was so excited that on the first day I couldn't eat breakfast.

The first run took an hour and a half. The entire group collapsed at the bottom. My legs burned; they felt tired and heavy. Everyone was gasping for air while the coach was attempting to gather us together. Then he let go with a sermon I'll never forget — "Legs that burn can't turn."

Early-day leg burn happens to skiers of all levels. Lack of proper preparation before you hit the hill has more to do with leg burn than lack of conditioning. Even the fittest skiers experience leg burn if they don't get in a routine before going skiing. Leg burn occurs because muscles are not getting enough oxygen.

- **Breakfast fuels the fire**

- **Breathing gives muscles oxygen**

- **Stretching loosens up muscles**

Start your day with three simple actions: eat, breathe, and stretch. Breakfast fuels the fire, breathing gives muscles oxygen, and stretching loosens up muscles. These three basic steps will help you enjoy your day on the slopes.

A good meal to start the day will give your body the fuel it needs to be active and stay warm. Food is essential for your body's furnace. Three solid meals with snacks in between are a must for anybody exercising in the mountains. Breakfast kick-starts your day; a snack around 10:30 rekindles the fire; lunch will help sustain your energy level; a mid-afternoon snack will keep your body alert as your muscles tire and your energy starts to fail.

Once on the lift, concentrate on the breathing process all the way to the top. This will relax you and fuel your muscles with oxygen. At the top of the lift, stretch again. Reach for the sky with your hands and arch your back at the same time. Continue to breathe at an even pace. Do this five times.

For your first run, take it slowly with three to four rest stops. Concentrate on breathing and enjoy the feeling of being on your skis. Look around and relax. Enjoy yourself and your surroundings. Try not to think about your style; it's more important to be loose and calm.

Next time up the lift, stretch. Reach for the sky and lean left to right slowly. Try to reach for your skis with your hands. Hold each stretch for a count of five and don't bounce. Keep your head up while stretching and be sure that you continue to concentrate on your breathing. This adds to the effectiveness of the stretch.

At the top, spread your legs shoulder-width apart and reach down and touch the snow, holding your head up, and count to ten. Then slowly reach up for the sky, count to ten, back down to the snow (don't bounce), count to ten, and reach for the sky. Repeat five times.

Oxygen is vital in order for our muscles to perform. Concentrate on breathing when you wake up. Do ten push-ups or ten sit-ups — anything to get your body awake and fresh oxygen into your system. On your way up the lift, focus on your breathing. You'll feel the difference immediately.

Cut cards with scissors or knife along perforations. Do not rip cards from binding.
Card surfaces are weatherproof. For best protection place clear tape over card edges.

5

Dan Egan's Chairlift Guide to Skiing
BALANCE - Foot Placement

GOAL:
The goal of this drill is to experience hip angulation during a skiing simulation.

BODY POSITION:
No skis, walk downhill making large radius turns.

Walk downhill, simulating short radius turns. Keep your upper body facing downhill and plant your poles as if you were skiing.

It is important to unweight between the turns. Unweighting on the traverse will allow your feet to move quickly.

Keep hips square to the hill and move feet away from the body, creating hip angulation. Use outside foot to make the turn.

Keep the upper body relaxed, arms out in a natural position, and head up with eyes looking downhill.

CARD 3A

3

Dan Egan's Chairlift Guide to Skiing
BALANCE - Ski Walking

GOAL:
Building balance, independent leg action and dynamic motion.

BODY POSITION:
March downhill, skis on but no poles.

Start skiing straight down the hill. Lift one leg off the snow at a time, as if you are marching.

Keep your upper body relaxed, hands in a natural position while you look down the hill.

Stay in control while you go a short distance. Focus on the flat ski on the snow.

This drill helps you become comfortable in a variety of dynamic positions.

CARD 2A

1

Dan Egan's Chairlift Guide to Skiing
BALANCE - The Gravity Pull

GOAL:
Learn the efficient use of your body in relation to gravity.

BODY POSITION:
No skis, walk downhill staying perpendicular to the slope.

On a gentle slope without skis; stand facing downhill.

Walk forward leading with your chest.

You will feel little weight or resistance on your feet. Roll your feet from the ball of your foot to your toes.

This drill maximizes your balance, which enhances your mobility and fluidity.

CARD 1A

Cut cards with scissors or knife along perforations. Do not rip cards from binding.
Card surfaces are weatherproof. For best protection place clear tape over card edges.

GOAL:
Develop knee angulation and upper body positioning in short radius turns.

BODY POSITION:
No skis, make small jump turns down the hill.

Make small jump turns. Jump sideways, slightly down the hill.

The key to knee angulation is keeping your hip and shoulders over your knees. Note the A-FRAME between the knees.

Spring up from your toes and land on the inside edge of the outside boot.

This drill develops independent leg action and quick foot movement.

3B

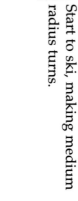

GOAL:
Learning to identify your center without relying on your boots.

BODY POSITION:
Large radius turns with boots unbuckled. Rock between your heel and toes.

Start to ski, making medium radius turns.

In between turns, stand up on your toes. As you turn, sink down on to your heels and drive your shins against the tongue of your boots.

Go slow: concentrate on feeling your feet in the boots.

This drill builds your confidence and raises your awareness of how your equipment works in relationship to your body.

2B

GOAL:
Experiencing the pull of gravity and the glide of a flat ski.

BODY POSITION:
Skis on, ski straight downhill staying perpendicular to the slope.

Start to ski, leading with your chest. Keep your head up and eyes forward.

Feel the acceleration and the weightlessness of your body.

When gravity pulls your body from the center, there is minimal effort and maximum efficiency.

This drill helps you gain greater awareness of gravity and its effects on your body.

1B

The Golden Rule of Skiing

The golden rule in skiing is "Ski the mountain, don't let the mountain ski you." This is the bottom line when it comes to skiing. To become a master of the mountain, learn to adapt to changing terrain, conditions, and speed. Always remember that you are the boss. A skier skis the mountain and doesn't let the mountain ski him or her.

Changes in terrain, conditions, and speed will bring out flaws in skiers' technique. Skiing is a constant realignment of balance. Teach yourself to constantly deal with changing terrain and to trust your current ability in order to progress.

> ### The Golden Rule of Skiing
>
> **Ski the mountain,
> don't let the mountain ski you.**

Find your own pace. Start by skiing at a constant speed all the time no matter what the conditions are. It is important to establish a skiing speed that is right for you. It should be determined by your ability to stop at any given moment. A good mogul skier, even after taking air, is able to stop on a dime. A racer skiing a slalom course possesses the ability to change direction at any given moment or else miss a gate.

Free skiing the mountain is no different. Find a speed that feels comfortable to you and begin and end your ski run at that same speed. Always make your first and last turns the best. The first turn will set up your confidence and rhythm for that set of turns. Making your last turn the best is an insurance policy against injury and laziness. Using this as a rule, you will find it easier to ski at a constant speed with more control.

Once you are able to ski at a *constant speed*, start to ski *changing terrain*. Ski directly into a trail without stopping on top. If you need to stop, pick a spot 15 to 20 yards into the trail. This will provide an excellent opportunity for learning to adapt speed and technique to changing terrain. Discover the magic of entering a trail without stopping, of turning and absorbing a knoll. Ski into and through an intersection in complete control and heads will turn as you ski away on a wide open slope.

Make skiing fun by challenging yourself. For example, get off the lift ready to ski, boots buckled, poles on, and ski right off the lift and down into your favorite trail. Then see how many turns you can make in a certain section of the trail, or try making 50 turns with the same radius and at the same speed. Use the terrain and mix up slalom and giant slalom turns. Remind yourself that it's your mountain, you rule the school, and anything goes if you so deem it!

One of my favorite drills is to ski top to bottom non-stop. Doing this a couple of times a day gets my adrenaline pumping and my awareness of my skiing ability increases. Skiing over changing terrain and adapting while in motion is the best teacher for your mind and body. Nothing can replace the experience gained by recovering your balance without stopping, or by making two big sweeping turns around a corner and then skiing the fall line through some bumps non-stop. Mountains will become less intimidating and skiers will begin to understand the fall line and conditions that cover the trail. Small trouble spots will pass by without a second thought and, most importantly, as ability improves, so does confidence.

Skiers who learn to adapt to changing terrain, conditions, and speed will enjoy more of what the mountain has to offer and will start to ski terrain they never thought possible before.

Balance

Cards 1 through 3

Balance is something we're all born with. It's instinctive and natural; we rarely have to consciously think about it. Basically, we were born to walk, run, skip, and jump. With this gift of balance comes *trust*, a subconscious trust of standing up and not falling over, whether we're walking, running, or participating in athletic activities.

With this natural sense of balance and trust in our natural abilities, we humans have been able to accomplish extraordinary athletic feats. The underlying theme of this multimedia learning package is that when you, the skier, are in balance, you will be able to achieve proper ski technique naturally.

Understanding the basic aspects of balance is the key to understanding how to ski. I can't stress this enough. Ruedi Bear wrote in his book, *Ski Like the Best*, "When you ski, never get locked into any kind of firm position." Skiing is a dynamic sport. It is disastrous for your skiing to become stuck in a static position.

We were born in balance, without having to take lessons or instructions. Children have an easier time learning balance sports, such as skiing or riding a bicycle, because they don't think about it – they just do it. The brain is good for many things, but at times it can act at cross-purposes with our natural instincts and abilities. It's only when our brain starts thinking about what we're doing that our natural instincts falter and the brain takes over. When that happens, we consciously *act*, instead of instinctively *reacting*. We try to take control and suddenly we find that we've gotten out of balance.

Many times, while skiing down a steep slope or through the mogul fields, I have recovered my balance by simply throwing my upper body down the fall line and letting my feet follow. It works almost every time when I trust that gravity, balance, and my natural instincts will work the way they are meant to.

The six drills that follow are the foundation you need to become reacquainted with your natural sense of balance on skis. They'll help you learn a new feeling of trust in yourself and your instinctive abilities. Take the time to work all the way through each of them, and perform all the recommended sets of each. Remember, each drill complements every other drill in the program, so build a good foundation and practice, practice, practice.

Gravity Pull

In her book *The Centered Skier*, Denise McCluggage says this: "What is an essential difference between a good skier and a poor skier? It is their relationship with the mountain." To form our relationship with the mountain, we have to understand gravity's effect on our bodies.

The reason most beginning skiers have trouble is that they haven't established a relationship to gravity. Too many things have changed at once. You're on a steep mountain slope, you're in the snow, and you're wearing skis and big clodhopper boots. To put this into perspective, think about what it would be like simply walking down that mountain.

Well, that's just what we're going to do with this drill. If you gotta crawl before you can walk, then you gotta walk before you can ski. We're going to take off our skis and walk down the mountain. We will establish a relationship with gravity and understand its pull on us – hence the name of this drill, GRAVITY PULL.

Goal: Learning the efficient use of our body in relation to gravity

Body Position: No skis; walk downhill staying perpendicular to the slope

In mastering this drill, you'll learn the efficient use of your body in relation to gravity. Simply put, this drill teaches you how to keep your body balanced at all times, no matter which direction you're skiing or how steep the slope. You'll begin learning how to enhance your mobility and fluidity. Remember, skiing is about constant fluidity. Any kind of rigidity is a no-no.

The first thing is to get yourself up a gentle slope with your boots on and your skis off. This is a drill you can do anywhere, which means you can do it in your back yard if you want to. Set your skis to one side, making sure your brakes are extended. Now turn and face down the hill. Stand up straight, your knee joints relaxed, and your back straight.

Next, pretend a rope has been tied around your chest and someone is pulling you downhill. Begin walking forward, leading with your chest. This will keep you perpendicular. Keep your head up, looking straight ahead. Your arms should be hanging loosely, slightly away from your sides.

Roll your feet inside your boots from the ball of your foot to your toes. You shouldn't feel much weight or resistance on your feet. Take easy, baby steps at first. As you gain confidence, move a little faster and lengthen your stride.

Perform this drill in two sets of five. Let your body really get into it! If you're doing this drill correctly, you'll feel how much easier it is to have motion moving down the hill when you're working with gravity, not against it. The reason we do this drill without skis is so that you won't be distracted or intimidated by the equipment and the awkwardness of having skis on your feet.

Remember, you're learning how to keep your body erect and perpendicular to the slope. Internalize how easily your feet move when gravity is pulling you from the center of your chest. This weightlessness on your feet will make it much easier for you to turn your skis.

Gravity Pull With Skis

In the previous drill, you experienced how you can use gravity to orient your body efficiently when walking downhill. If you did two sets of repetitions, you probably have a very good feel for it now. In this drill, we're going to practice the GRAVITY PULL WITH SKIS to see how gravity works when we're actually on our skis.

Use the same, gentle slope to practice this drill. Put on your skis and face downhill in a snowplow stop. Now start to ski straight down the hill, leading with your chest. This will keep you perpendicular to the slope. As before, be sure to keep your head up and your eyes looking forward.

Goal: Experiencing the pull of gravity and the glide of a flat ski

Body Position: Skis on; ski straight downhill staying perpendicular to the slope

As you start to move, you'll immediately feel a sense of acceleration, combined with a feeling of weightlessness on your feet. You'll almost feel as if you're gliding through the air. On the video you will clearly see acceleration. This is due to the way you're holding your body. You allow gravity to pull your body forward, from your chest, while keeping yourself erect and centered. Gravity does all the work for you. You exert minimal effort, yet will get maximum efficiency in return. Go for 20-30 feet, then stop.

This drill is a great way to learn how the flat ski feels and performs when your body is perpendicular to the slope. It's the natural way to accelerate. I like this drill because it's a way to conserve energy and be efficient. I often find it is the best way — especially when I'm tired — to let gravity and balance get me down the hill.

Ski Walking

Ski Walking is a natural extension of our learned walking skills. This drill teaches mobility, because a mobile skier will stay in balance longer and will be able to handle greater changes in terrain. It builds upon the balancing exercises you've been practicing, and you'll learn how to be more agile on a flat ski.

In skiing, both legs must be totally independent. As well, your legs and your upper body must be independent of each other. This drill teaches your body this independent relationship, which will greatly enhance your performance.

Skiing is the art of seeing where you want to put your feet and your skis, then putting them there. This is called foot placement, and it's critical to successful mountain skiing. In order to master foot placement, you must first learn to be mobile. Ski walking is another step — no pun intended! — toward greater mobility. You'll learn that while you're in motion, you can lift a foot off the snow while still skiing on the other. Later you'll see that by lifting one foot and then the other, you can easily change the line you're skiing down the slope. This is a very important skill and one that quickly builds your confidence.

> **Goal: Building balance, independent leg action, and dynamic motion**
>
> **Body Position: March downhill, skis on but no poles**

17

Begin by positioning yourself on a gentle slope, facing downhill. Set your poles aside so you can experience a natural sense of balance with your arms. If you'd like a dry run first, stand still on a flat surface with your hands out, palms down, and raise each leg in turn until your knee contacts your palm, as illustrated in the video. Now start skiing straight ahead while looking down the hill, keeping your skis flat, and march as you ski.

Maintain that balanced, relaxed upper body position you learned in the previous drills. Now, lift one foot off the snow and hold it in the air for a few seconds, then slowly set it back down. Ski for a few seconds, then lift the other foot, holding it as you did the other, before setting it back down. You will gain speed, so don't go too far, and make sure the slope is not too crowded.

Be sure that you keep your hands and arms in a comfortable, relaxed position to help maintain your balance. Ski just a short distance and maintain your focus. Keep your gaze set downhill and your skis flat on the snow. Make sure that the tip of your ski does not raise higher than the toe of your boot. If anything, point your tip down below your toe. This will keep you leaning forward.

Repeat this drill ten times. I often practice it on a traverse to a different trail or lift. It will help you become comfortable in a variety of dynamic positions – and, as you may have guessed, dynamic positions are what downhill skiing is all about!

Unbuckled Boots

In skiing, balance is the one ingredient that everyone must have in order to reach new levels in ability. Moreover, it's the one element that is instinctive to every human being. We all have it and, on skis, we can all find it — if we stop relying on our equipment and start relying on our natural abilities. To improve as a skier, it is critical to discover your natural balance on skis.

The best drill for discovering natural balance on skis is to ski with your ski boots unbuckled. Do this mid-morning after stretching and warming up. This ensures good circulation down to the toes and keeps your feet warm. Take a couple of runs on a slope that is below your ability level. Latch your boot buckles as loosely as possible. Skiing in this fashion will force you to find the natural balance point on skis at all times. No longer relying on the safeguard and support of the boots, natural instinct will make adjustments in your skiing stance that will allow your body to remain balanced.

Goal: Learning to identify your center without relying on your boots

Body Position: Make large radius turns with boots unbuckled; rock back and forth between your heels and toes

You can begin practicing this drill in your living room or ski condo before you actually head out to ski. Slip into your boots and latch the buckles loosely. Now stand in skiing position and push your knees forward. You should feel your shins press into the boot tongue while rocking between your toes and heels. Move your body from the hips down as if you were actually skiing and give your boots a real workout as you flex in them. Watching the video will help you get the rhythm and movement and you'll feel your *feet* – not your boots – as they move.

Now you're ready to try this on the slopes. Snap into your bindings with your boots still loosely buckled and begin skiing. Make easy, medium radius turns. Go slowly while trying this – it may feel slightly out of control at first, making turns difficult. Start off making wide, sweeping giant slalom turns until your confidence grows. Next, start to ski more down the fall line, making sharper, shorter turns.

A common mistake during this exercise occurs when the skier concentrates too much on the fact that his or her boots are unbuckled rather than on how to stay balanced. Forget about your feet and focus on standing in the middle of your skis in an athletic stance with feet shoulder-width apart, hands and shoulders square to the hill. Remain flexible and adapt your body to the changing terrain. Stay forward in your boots by curling your toes. That one little action will bring your whole body forward and allow you to stand strong, balanced, and in the center of the skis. The old saying "Keep on your toes" applies in every sport and skiing is no different. When we are on our toes, we are mobile and ready to move in any direction – critical in skiing.

Arms and hands play a huge part in a balanced ski stance. Keep upper body movement very limited. A good tip to remember is that if you can't see both arms at the same time, then they are out of position. Don't confuse a quiet, strong upper body with a stiff and tense upper body. The biggest benefits in raising your skill level come when you are relaxed and fluid, calm and strong.

Your comfort level will grow after a couple of runs. Often, I will forget that my boots are unbuckled! When that happens, progress is being made. Subconsciously, I am adjusting my stance on my skis and trusting my natural instincts more. At this point, take on more challenging terrain, progress slowly and continue making wide, sweeping giant slalom turns until your confidence grows. Then start to ski more in the fall line with shorter radius turns. More advanced skiers may want to venture into the moguls or steeps. Keep in mind that a change in terrain or speed will magnify your mistakes, making you more aware of how your body becomes out of balance. Test yourself, but be safe and consider the skiers around you.

This is an awareness drill. Note your body position and remember: When it's hard to turn, you're out of balance; when it's easy to turn, you're in balance. Pay attention to the differences and start to notice which parts of your body affect your balance. I find the best way to improve is to let my mind relax and enjoy the beauty of the mountains. I never do one drill all day long. To me, skiing is fun, and getting better is just one reason to do drills.

Just before lunch, buckle up your boots and enjoy a slow run down to the lodge. During lunch, rest for at least a half hour because the muscles normally supported by boots have been working extra hard. After lunch, buckle up and go for a good ski. Use the rest of the day to build awareness of your body and what it takes to stay balanced. By improving your balance, you will gain confidence in your skiing skill and skiing will become a more enjoyable experience.

Foot Placement

You may be wondering why, up until this point, we have not discussed turning. Rather, all of our movements have been straight down the hill. This is because it is important for you to gain a sense of your body moving down the fall line. When you ski in the fall line, gravity does its share of the work and you save energy.

However, the time has come to start turning, but once again without skis. Before we can ski and turn, we must begin to understand body position and the two basic ways to pressure the edges of our skis. They are hip angulation and knee angulation.

Goal: To experience hip angulation during a skiing simulation

Body Position: No skis; walk downhill making large radius turns

The FOOT PLACEMENT drill is designed to illustrate hip angulation through ski simulation while walking downhill. Begin by facing downhill with your skis off, but using your poles. Now, begin walking downhill, making large radius turns. Use your poles for balance and remember to pole plant between turns. Move on an imaginary axis; as you complete the arc, begin a turn in the other direction so that you're making a continuous S turn.

Take small steps: it is important to discover how both feet play a role in skiing. The goal is to have two independent legs constantly moving to create a mobile, fluid, athletic stance. Feel the power and stability generated by the downhill foot, the ease and grace of the transition onto the uphill foot. Together, but moving separately, two legs create stability.

What you will notice is that in between turns you are standing tall, or unweighting, and in the middle of the turn, you are sinking down, or weighting, lowering your hips. Your feet are out away from your body. Weighting is most evident in the belly of the turn. This action is clearly shown in the video and on the card.

To do this drill correctly, think about the edges of your boots like the edges of your skis. They need to dig into the snow. The only time you will walk on a flat boot is in between turns, which is the time of unweighting.

During the turn, the downhill boot is the most important. The inside edge of the downhill boot is your foundation for stability. The uphill boot is the transition boot. In other words, finish your turns on the downhill leg; in between turns, step up onto the uphill leg; unweight; step downhill and begin to turn again. You should feel a natural progression of foot placement.

Repeat this drill 6-8 times. Do it until you feel as if you are skiing. Trust in gravity and your natural balance to find proper foot placement. If you stumble, that's gravity and balance speaking to you. Check two things: First, are your boots on edge? Second, are you standing tall in between turns and sinking down in the turn?

Hip angulation is used in large radius turns because it keeps you stable at higher speeds. The important elements in this drill are to keep your body facing and moving downhill while your feet move out away from your body.

By now, you are feeling the ease with which your body moves *down* the fall line while your feet move *across* the fall line. This is important because it builds confidence and allows for a more balanced, mobile, athletic stance.

Jump Turn Without Skis

This drill is a great warm-up for a day of skiing. It focuses on knee angulation, isolation and separation of body parts, radius turns, foot placement, and pole plants all together in a real test of what you've learned. In doing so, it is a great way to improve your coordination.

JUMP TURN WITHOUT SKIS develops knee angulation and upper body positioning while you're making short radius turns. Begin this drill by facing downhill with your skis off, but using your poles. Make small jump turns as you leap a short distance into the air. Your lead leg should move slightly sideways and down the slope as you do so.

Goal: Learning to develop knee angulation and upper body position during short radius turns

Body Position: No skis; make small jump turns down the hill

Use your poles to keep yourself in position. The key to this drill is keeping your body perpendicular – your hips and shoulders directly over your knees. In the previous lesson, you learned hip angulation. Now you are learning knee angulation. Your body – from your shoulders to your knees – is moving as a harmonious whole.

Study the images on the card and video to see the effectiveness of the A-FRAME and knee angulation in short radius turns.

Spring up from your toes and land on the inside edge of your outside boot and spring up again. Soon you'll feel how this drill develops independent leg action and quick response in your feet. This is important in skiing smoothly over changing terrain.

Practice this drill in two or three sets of ten. It's a real test of how well you're progressing in your drills, and it's a great warm-up as well!

Upper Body

Cards 4 through 7

I've learned a lot about upper body position from Mihaela. The following stories of her early years in Romania clearly paint images of why upper body positioning has added to her success in skiing.

"In my early years traveling with my ski club in Romania, we stayed in the mountains for months and, in our free time, I taught my teammates how to do back flips. I knew how to do them because I grew up in the Nadia Comaneci era, and everyone took gymnastic lessons.

The most important principle I learned in gymnastics was that the body follows the head and that our hands are the tools that guide the body around. Understanding this principle has helped me in every sport I have learned, including skiing.

If you want to ski at your potential, you must learn to have a calm upper body. If you don't, you may start to move in directions you don't want to go. Any extra movement in your upper body will throw off your balance. The simple rule is to let your head and eyes take you where you want to go and let your body follow with a calm and strong upper body.

Sometimes language is the key. So often I have found when learning a new sport that all the information exists, but I just don't get it. Then someone will say the magic word or phrase and – bingo – I grab it.

In basketball class, the teacher taught me to dribble the ball just off to one side of my body. This allows hand movement to be lateral while at the same time out in front. Plus she would yell, 'Keep the ball where you can see it.'

The same is true in skiing. We plant our poles in front of our body and slightly off to the side. This keeps our hands where we can see them and allows them to guide our body through changes in terrain and conditions. So when you ski, keep your hands and arms relaxed, out in front, and slightly off to the side."

The drills in this section will help you achieve this goal. LOOK DOWN THE HILL teaches you to look beyond obstacles and down the hill. POLE CLAPPING and HAND CLAPPING will teach you to "keep 'em where you can see 'em." BE A BIRD is a fun drill that teaches you that laughing at yourself can be good for your skiing. POLE POINT and MOGUL POLE are the two most important pole planting drills in this package. DOWNHILL HAND PRESSURE and DOWNHILL HAND SWEEP both illustrate the importance of the upper body and how it relates to the lower body.

Remember, the more economical your movements, the less energy wasted. This will make you more efficient and allow you to ski at your potential.

LOOK DOWN THE HILL

It is important to maximize the relationship between yourself and the mountain. This drill will bring you one step closer to understanding that relationship and realizing how your eyes play a big part in interpreting what is to be skied. Skiers at all abilities cannot afford to be startled by obstacles or changes in terrain. Our eyes are the tool that prepares our senses for what lies ahead. Learn how to better utilize this tool and you will learn to overcome fear of steeper slopes, changing snow conditions, and obstacles.

The LOOK DOWN THE HILL drill will get your body into the proper position for good skiing. Your shoulders will be straight, your arms out in front of your body, and your head facing straight ahead so that you are looking down the hill. Your attention will be focused on your goal. Don't let the simplicity of this drill fool you. Looking down the hill has many benefits; for instance, your body will go where you look. If you look off to the side, you aren't skiing downhill any longer and you'll be focusing on the wrong things.

Goal: To illustrate that your body goes where you look

Body Position: Ski with your head up and eyes looking down the fall line

Extreme Team member Dean Decas, better known as the Dean of Skiing, says, "The biggest improvement I see in skiers is when they learn to look down the hill and look past obstacles that used to cause them fear or disrupt their focus."

29

Start this drill on any slope you're comfortable with and face downhill. Begin skiing and make sure that your head is pointed downhill and your eyes are looking straight down the fall line. Your head is the key to athletic motion and looking ahead will square your shoulders to the hill. This is the best position for your body. The video and card show the eyes looking down the hill as the body moves to get into the best skiing position.

Now begin to traverse. Let your skis run across the hill, but keep your head up and your eyes looking down the fall line. As you begin to make your turn, swing your body to face downhill to align with your eyes. Continue looking down the fall line as you begin to traverse in the opposite direction. Feel how your eyes guide you.

The interesting thing about letting our body follow our gaze is that we intuitively and automatically follow the fall line and the path of least resistance. This enhances our relationship with the mountain and smoothes out our skiing style without any major adjustments to our skiing technique. Once again, this proves that when our body is in the right position, skiing becomes easier.

So now you have a new tool to use in order to overcome fear of an obstacle or changes in snow conditions. Just look past it, look beyond to where you want to go – which is downhill. This active visualization will help you get your eyes focused down the hill so that you ski exactly where you want to go.

POLE CLAPPING

I call ski poles "Twizzle Sticks," because many skiers don't realize what their poles are really supposed to be used for. As a result, ski poles can actually get in the way of a relaxed, fluid style of skiing. POLE CLAPPING is a drill that will give you a better sense of how to use your poles. As you practice it, you will learn more about the concept of isolation and separation of body parts. You'll find out where your hands and arms are – and where they're supposed to be. You will also learn the importance of your

> **Goal: To develop constant fluid motion and isolation and separation of certain body parts**
>
> **Body Position: Ski, clicking your poles instead of pole plants**

hand position in relation to your overall balance. This is the beginning of seeing the positive effects of gentle, subtle movements versus jerky, wild, disruptive reactions. And you'll get a much better sense of how you can use your poles to ski better.

Begin skiing down any slope you're comfortable with. Once you're moving, begin making short radius turns. Once you're in the turn, raise your arms in front of you and cross your poles, clicking them together as they cross. As you make the X with your poles, look at the position of your hands. The video clearly shows the natural hand position: they're out in front of your body, exactly where they should be. Your head and eyes are pointed downhill.

31

Next time you cross and clap, feel the position of your shoulders. They are square with the hill and your body is pointed directly downhill, on the fall line. Once again, this is exactly where everything should be.

Continue your pole claps. Notice that all the motion of clicking the poles and making the X is in your wrists. Similarly, whenever you make a pole plant, the motion should all be in your wrist.

This is what we mean by the separation and isolation of body parts. Once you see and feel where the individual parts are, integrate them back into your whole body sense. Combine what you're doing in the drill with a smooth, fluid motion. Put it all together and feel yourself skiing better. This drill takes the focus off skiing technique and places it on your natural ability. Internalize the isolation and separation of your whole body from your feet, knees, and hips right through to your head, shoulders, and hands.

Have fun with pole clapping. Create your own clapping rhythm while you ski — it helps you gain more confidence. Even more importantly, it helps you see that you can make quicker and gentler pole plants. You don't need to stab at the snow. A light touch is much more efficient and helps minimize effort and movement.

HAND CLAPPING

Now that you've become comfortable with pole clapping, let's set the poles aside and spend some time skiing without them. It's easier than you might think and the benefits are great: You'll learn how to keep your upper body still and in position and you will continue to develop better hand positioning.

Most athletes instinctively know where to put their hands when they're exercising. Holding onto poles can interfere with this natural positioning. Take a look at snowboarders and notice how gracefully they use their arms and hands – almost like dancers. Because they're not holding anything, they instinctively use their hands for balance and positioning. We'll use this drill to learn how to use our hands the same way.

> **Goal: To develop upper body positioning and natural hand positioning**
>
> **Body Position: Ski without poles and clap where you would pole plant**

Begin skiing down a slope you're comfortable with. Put your hands out in front of you in a natural position. As you make your turns, hold your arms and hands out for proper balance, as you would if you were holding your poles. Right at the end of your turn, clap your hands as if you're congratulating yourself on that fine turn you're making. As with POLE CLAPPING, seek out your own natural rhythm for HAND CLAPPING. As you turn, straighten and clap; turn, straighten and clap; you'll feel a new confidence in your skiing. This comes from your upper body being in proper position. You're not using your poles as – excuse the term – crutches.

You'll also experience a new sense of freedom, because you're in natural balance. You're not using your pole plants to balance yourself; instead you're using your own natural sense of balance. This new freedom is contagious and can be seen on the video. Remember to keep your head up and eyes looking down the hill. Combining these two new skills will allow you to make lighter and more effective pole plants, which will result in the ability to ski all sorts of exciting new slopes.

Spend a morning skiing without poles, practicing the HAND CLAPPING drill. Then go out after lunch with your poles and see what a difference it makes! Perhaps more than any other drill, skiing without poles will help you correct most of your upper body mistakes.

BE A BIRD

I love to sit and watch birds fly and glide; they move so effortlessly — it seems as if they can fly for hours and hours on end. A bird soaring high in the mountains has become my ultimate visualization for how I want to ski. I often use visualization to relax my mind and body. When I'm relaxed, I'm able to concentrate on using just the muscles needed at a specific time and place within a turn. The result is less effort needed to complete the turn. Birds have mastered the most efficient way to utilize their bodies' features with the task at hand.

This drill has three main elements – gliding, sliding, and carving. To improve, skiers must search for the most efficient way to combine all three elements. The easiest way to link the elements together is to relax and let your body float down the hill.

Goal: To enhance the feeling of constant, fluid motion

Body Position: Ski straight downhill while flapping your wings 3 times and then make 3 turns

Birds have mastered the most efficient way to utilize their body's features with the task at hand. So, put your poles aside and flap your arms, just as a bird does, and fly down the slopes. As you do this drill, you are enhancing the feeling of constant, fluid motion, which will make you more mobile plus give your body the ability to adjust to changes in speed, conditions, and terrain.

35

Find a smooth gentle slope you're comfortable on – a private one if you're worried that other skiers will think you've gone wacky! – and ski straight down the fall line, flapping your arms in the air just like a bird. Stand tall and allow yourself to be pulled by gravity, similar to the GRAVITY PULL WITH SKIS. Picture yourself floating just above the snow, being pulled by gravity, and turning wherever you like.

Have fun! Loosen up! A big smile and a hearty laugh will speed you on your way. Notice the smile on Mihaela's face in the video.

Flap your arms two or three times, then begin a turn. As you do so, you'll feel your downhill arm and leg moving together. Let your feet move under your knees and your knees move under your hips in a smooth, gliding motion. Your downhill arm will point down the hill while your uphill arm will remain raised. Think of how a bird or an airplane makes a turn, tipping a wing and gliding in the downward direction. You'll feel your body gracefully do the same thing.

This drill reinforces the fact that you don't need poles for balance and turning. Your body is truly in control at all times; the poles are simply guides and helpers. Repeat this drill until you actually feel as if you are floating. Your turns should be effortless and smooth. Any sort of jerking motion is a signal to do it again.

This is a very relaxing and rewarding drill. Enjoy it, and please, remember to smile. Smiling sends a message to your whole body to enjoy what you're doing. Remember, skiing is recreation, not work, so smile and relax!

POLE POINT

Now that you've practiced skiing without poles to learn proper hand, arm, and upper body position, you can learn how to use the poles properly. The POLE POINT drill is intended to do just that. In this drill, you'll combine what you've learned in all the previous Upper Body drills.

Get yourself into position on a comfortable slope with your hands holding your poles out in front of your body in a nice, relaxed position. Now, point your index fingers downhill, right at the place where you're looking. Keep your head up, shoulders square to the hill.

Goal: To develop a proper pole plant and hand position

Body Position: Hold your poles with both index fingers pointing down the fall line

Begin skiing the fall line. As you move forward, extend the tip of one pole by cocking your wrist so that your index finger points up in the air. Then plant the tip of the pole in the snow gently. As you do so, your index finger will level out. Ski by the tip of the pole so that your index finger is pointing down at the snow. When you're ready to turn, repeat the motion with the other pole. You don't need to swing your whole upper body or stab at the snow. The important motion is the snap of the wrist. Keep your index fingers pointed to give you a reference for the proper motion.

Develop a smooth, easy motion as illustrated in the video, using your wrists, not your shoulders. Plant one pole tip, then move your arm forward to the extent of

37

your reach. Then point the opposite pole tip out in front of your body and repeat the motion. Chant this mantra: point, plant, push.

Continue this smooth, rhythmic motion until you have a natural feeling of wrist movement. Notice how your shoulders stay square to the hill and do not rotate. Notice how your arms stay bent in a relaxed way and move forward and backward as your poles and index fingers point the way down the hill. Keep pointing until the motion is burned into your mind. You can practice this motion on or off the snow. Mastering this drill will allow you to use your poles instinctively.

POLE POINT further emphasizes the isolation and separation of body parts – in this case, the arms and wrists. Notice how, because of the previous drills where you did not use your poles, they have become a natural extension of your body. Notice also that when you didn't use your poles, you held your hands out in front of your body. This drill reminds you to always keep your hands out in front where you can see them and use them. You'll now be skiing more naturally, and your body will have the confidence to relax and enjoy skiing.

Cut cards with scissors or knife along perforations. Do not rip cards from binding.
Card surfaces are weatherproof. For best protection place clear tape over card edges.

UPPER BODY – Look Down The Hill
1

GOAL:
To illustrate that your body goes where you look.

BODY POSITION:
Ski with your head up and eyes looking down the fall line.

Ski with your head up, eyes looking down the fall line.

When traversing, let your skis run across the hill but keep your eyes looking down the fall line.

Turn with upper body square to the hill, keep your eyes looking down the fall line

You will go where you look. Keeping your head up and eyes looking down the hill, to follow the path of least resistance.

CARD 4A

UPPER BODY – Hand Clapping
3

GOAL:
To develop upper body positioning and natural hand positioning.

BODY POSITION:
Ski without poles and clap when you would pole plant.

Make a series of short radius turns.

Clap your hands once between turns to give yourself more confidence.

Notice the natural shoulder and hand positioning.

Skiing without poles helps you discover a new feeling of freedom and improved balance.

CARD 5A

UPPER BODY – Pole Point
5

GOAL:
To develop a proper pole plant and hand position.

BODY POSITION:
Hold your poles with both index fingers always pointing down the fall line.

Start to ski facing downhill. Hold both poles with index fingers pointing down the fall line.

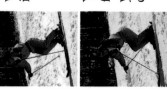

As you start the pole plant, lead with the tip of the pole

Plant your pole and push your wrist forward, keeping your index finger pointed.

Your wrist should end up in front of the ski pole tip with your index finger pointing down toward the slope.

CARD 6A

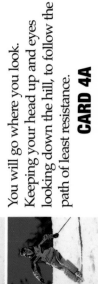

Cut cards with scissors or knife along perforations. Do not rip cards from binding. Card surfaces are weatherproof. For best protection place clear tape over card edges.

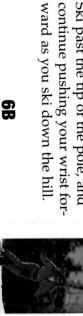
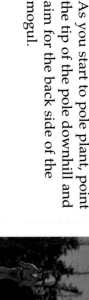

GOAL:
To develop quick pole plants in moguls.

BODY POSITION:
Hold both poles with index fingers pointing down the fall line.

Start to ski facing downhill. Hold both poles with index fingers pointing down the fall line.

As you start to pole plant, point the tip of the pole downhill and aim for the back side of the mogul.

Plant the pole on the back side of the mogul, push your wrist forward and point your body down the fall line.

Ski past the tip of the pole, and continue pushing your wrist forward as you ski down the hill.

6B

GOAL:
To enhance the feeling of constant, fluid motion.

BODY POSITION:
Ski straight downhill while flapping your wings three times and then make three turns.

Ski in a straight line and flap your arms three times, like a bird. Begin turning.

As you start to turn, let your hands fall into a natural position.

Keep your shoulders square to the hill and head up, eyes looking down the hill.

Let your feet move under your hips and knees while your hands imitate wings.

5B

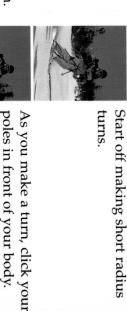

GOAL:
The goal of this drill is to develop constant fluid motion and isolation and separation of certain body parts.

BODY POSITION:
Ski, clicking your poles instead of planting them.

Start off making short radius turns.

As you make a turn, click your poles in front of your body. Keep the motion in your wrists.

Note that your hands are in the correct position and your shoulders are square to the hill.

Cross your poles and click between every turn. This helps you make quicker and lighter pole plants.

4B

MOGUL POLE

This drill moves all the Upper Body drills to a new level as you begin skiing more challenging terrain: the mogul fields. Now you're going to see how effective pole pointing can be.

Mogul skiing depends on a quiet upper body. Watch the video and you'll see Mihaela's and my legs pumping like pistons, but our upper bodies are calm, upright, and facing straight down the fall line. MOGUL POLE helps you learn how to use your poles to maintain upper body poise while your feet and skis are flying over and around moguls.

> **Goal: To develop quick pole plants in moguls**
>
> **Body Position: Hold both poles with index fingers pointing down the fall line**

Quick, precise pole plants are essential to successful mogul skiing. Begin skiing a small mogul field that is not too steep. Be sure your upper body is facing downhill, with your arms out in front of your body, holding your poles easily, your index fingers pointing down the fall line. The goal is to focus on your pole plants and not worry about turning.

Cameron Boyle, who is a three-time World Pro Mogul Champion, believes that the most important element in mogul skiing is the pole plant. In 1989, his first year on the tour, I saw Cameron practicing and visualizing his pole plants at his first event at Heavenly Valley on the lift and in the starting area before each run. Cameron not only won that event but the overall tour for the next two years.

Plant a pole and then use the same movement you learned in POLE PLANT. The action is point, plant, and push. Move your wrist forward as you aim for the back side of the mogul. You should always have your hands in sight. Always plant or try to plant the tip of your pole on the back side of the mogul. If you plant on the front side, you will jam your pole plant and, as you ski by the pole, your arm will be forced out to the side and beyond your body. Planting on the back side has many benefits. One, it allows natural hand and arm movement. Two, it keeps your shoulders square to the hill. Three, it allows the skier to better anticipate the next mogul. And four, it forces the skier to reach down the hill which will keep the body perpendicular to the hill.

Leverage your body up and over the mogul. Ski from the back to the front of the mogul, always maintaining a continuous, dynamic motion. Chant this mantra: point, plant, push.

You should be experiencing a flowing sensation as you ski with your pole plants from one mogul to the next. Notice how smoothly and quickly Mihaela and I move from bump to bump. Remember to point your finger to drive home the point of this drill. Keep your speed down so that you can concentrate on your pole plants.

Continue this drill until you feel confident on the small mogul field, then increase the intensity – either on more challenging terrain or by skiing at a higher rate of speed. Ski like the pros. Concentrate on your hands and your feet will follow. Your skiing skills will improve dramatically!

DOWNHILL HAND PRESSURE

Remember the soaring and turning hand movements you learned in BE A BIRD? This drill will show you the practical application of the movements and positioning.

The downhill hand position is critical in maintaining proper body position and works in conjunction with the downhill ski. Your upper body should always be perpendicular to the slope. Practice the DOWNHILL HAND PRESSURE drill to make sure that it is. Proper downhill hand positioning will keep your upper body over your feet. The result is a balanced athletic stance.

Begin skiing downhill, body upright and arms out and away from your body, like wings. Now begin making wide radius turns. Do not plant your poles.

> **Goal: To illustrate the importance of the downhill hand and arm and how they translate pressure to your lower body**
>
> **Body Position: Around every turn, pretend someone is pulling on your downhill hand, trying to pull you down the hill**

As you begin a turn, pretend that someone is pulling on your downhill arm. As you enter the middle of the turn, your downhill shoulder should be over your downhill ski. Your legs are bent and your hip is angulated. You should be able to draw a perfectly straight line from your ankle to your head. Watch Mihaela pulling my downhill hand in the video. This clearly illustrates the effect of downhill hand pressure.

Lead with your downhill arm, keeping it stretched out. Keep your head up and your eyes looking downhill. The pulling motion will actually guide you effortlessly into and out of your radius turns. You'll have that awesome experience of constant fluid motion in your skiing. This upper body steering will illustrate the connection between upper and lower body.

As you finish a turn and straighten out, unweight your downhill leg and bring your downhill hand forward. Initiate the next turn by switching the pressure to the opposite hand. Again, pretend someone is pulling on that hand. Keep it reaching out. Move your downhill hand out in front as if you were going to make a pole plant, but let it continue to glide instead. Continue this drill several more times until you can clearly feel the control your upper body has over the lower body.

On more challenging terrain, or when you're skiing fast, the DOWNHILL HAND PRESSURE drill becomes even more important. Yet all the motions and body positions are exactly the same as when you're making easy turns. Notice again the isolation and separation of body parts – the upper body providing stability while the lower body does all the work – producing the graceful and effortless skiing we all seek. On the steeps, upper body position is everything. The only way to stay mobile is to keep your upper body over your hips, knees, and feet. This positioning will keep your whole body perpendicular to the slope which creates the proper angle for all-terrain skiing.

DOWNHILL HAND SWEEP

Many skiers, not knowing better, ski with their feet and legs. No wonder they're tired and exhausted by lunchtime! What they don't realize is this: Upper body rules!

The lower body goes where the upper body orients it to go. Mastering the upper body is the breakthrough point in learning to ski better. Your upper body helps your balance, provides power, sustains your fluid motion, and initiates agility.

You saw how you can guide your movement in the DOWNHILL HAND PRESSURE drill. This drill, the DOWNHILL HAND SWEEP, extends that guidance. The movements you'll make here will amaze you. It's almost like doing yoga while you're skiing! The goal of this drill is to exaggerate the upper body movement to illustrate how it rules over the lower body. By the time you are done with this drill, you will understand how proper body mechanics are more important than ski technique. I have boosted hundreds of intermediate skiers into the

Goal: To illustrate how proper positioning of the upper body will completely control the lower body

Body Position: Ski making large radius turns; during the turn, sweep your downhill hand past your boot

next level through this drill. Mastering this drill helps you forget about foot steering, ankle pressure, and all the other terms that clog the mind. Focus instead on your body movement. Watch the video and you will see how the upper body rules over the feet and legs. When skiers complete this drill and look back at their tracks and see how smooth and round their turns are, they believe in proper body position as the key to better skiing!

Begin skiing down a wide slope where you can make big, easy radius turns. Begin a traverse and raise your arms nearly up to shoulder level. Now, concentrate only on your arms as you move your uphill shoulder around. You'll feel yourself beginning to turn. Reach downhill with your hand as if you were going to touch your boot. At the same time, reach up into the air with your other hand.

Continue sweeping your hand past your boot throughout the turn and back up into the original position. At the same time, continue bringing your uphill hand into the downhill sweep, reversing the direction of your turn. Reach for your boot again and sweep your hand back up to the original position. The sweeping motion creates momentum; the bending motion forces you to bend your knees and pressure your boots and skis. Sweeping your hand past your downhill boot and back to the original position unweights your skis and allows you to finish your turn with the tail of your skis. The result is a smooth, round turn with dynamic body movement. This movement keeps skiers in an athletic mobile stance while in constant motion.

If this reminds you of BE A BIRD, you're right. You're learning how to fly down the slopes! Remember to keep your upper body straight, your shoulders square to the hill, and your eyes facing downhill.

As you perform one downhill hand sweep after another, you'll begin to feel the grace of making smooth, rounded turns. This exercise is designed to illustrate upper body positioning in all-terrain skiing.

Power

It has been said that the essence of skiing is in the turn; the turn is the time and space when your body experiences a mix of forces. Centrifugal force, gravity, friction, and acceleration all come together to create a power only skiers can feel.

This elemental power is sometimes fluid and graceful and, at other times, explosive and dynamic. The power in skiing is hidden within the skier. Each individual shapes his or her own outcome and leaves behind only a path through the snow.

Many skiers come away from skiing a well-groomed Blue Square or an intensely demanding Black Diamond not feeling tired but exhilarated and filled with the power of skiing. Hours later, driving home, they still feel this power and will carry it back into their daily life as a sustaining feeling of empowerment.

The best explanation I've heard is that this elemental power is a feeling of being alive. I think Mihaela sums it up best: "People often comment about a picture of me ski racing and say, 'Wow, you look different there.' But of course I do. When I put my skis on, I'm a different person. I feel an unexplainable joy and happiness and, after so many years, I still manage to love it. It gives me a confident feeling about myself that stays with me in everything I do."

In the first two sections of this book, you were getting your body to perform. Now that you know something about balance and have learned about the importance

45

of the upper body, you are ready to add power to your stance and skiing positions.

In this section, you'll focus first on the elements of a powerful stance in the POWER POSITION and POWER POSITION TURN drills. Then you'll begin focusing on the ski. You'll master three techniques – sliding, edging, and carving – which make up the foundation of controlling your skis.

The POWER SLIDE drill teaches the importance of a flat ski and what it feels like to slide a ski. The POWER SLIDE TO TRAVERSE teaches the difference between a sliding and an edged ski and the POWER SLIDE TO TURN illustrates the difference between edging and carving.

The POWER TURN and the JACK RABBIT TURN are two drills that combine every element in this book. Mastering these two drills will build your confidence to a new level. Learning the techniques in this section will prepare you to enter the Zone of Excellence.

POWER POSITION

The POWER POSITION drill identifies how power in skiing is generated. The most important lesson in this drill is that the POWER POSITION changes throughout the turn. Therefore, skiers must sustain a mobile athletic stance throughout the entire phase of the turn. This drill is designed to make skiers realize that the POWER POSITION is a roaming, movable position. To be powerful, you cannot and must not be standing rigid.

This drill sets the tone for all of the power drills. Skiers who are balanced with quiet upper bodies are on their way to becoming powerful skiers. While you practice this drill, concentrate on feeling the flow of your movements. Be relaxed, but also dynamic and explosive. The POWER POSITION drill helps you develop an athletic stance that you'll use when you're in constant fluid motion.

> **Goal: To define your Power Position as an athletic stance in constant fluid motion**
>
> **Body Position: Stand in an athletic position on a flat surface with skis on; jump up and down 3 times.**

You won't even need a slope to perform this drill. Instead, find a flat area where you can stand with your skis on. Place your skis shoulder-width apart and your hands out in front. Now crouch down, then jump straight up in the air. Make sure your skis clear the ground, but keep them parallel to each other and perpendicular to the ground.

When you land, let your entire body compress. Bend your knees and bring your upper body down all the way. Absorb the entire landing and then jump up. Do three jumps.

Where is the POWER POSITION, you ask? Well, it is between the time you spring up to begin your jump and when the absorption of the landing is through. That whole range of movement is considered the POWER POSITION. Why? Because no one stage of the jump can exist without the prior stage. In other words, if you don't bend down, you can't effectively jump up and, if you don't extend in the air, you won't have a maximum height and, if you don't absorb the landing, you will have a jerky landing. Each stage relies on the next.

Power surrounds the whole act. Position is our ability to place our body in the right place at the right time. Power positions exist within the total movement of our body when we ski. The aim of this drill is to utilize your body positions for maximum power.

Do at least three sets of three or four POWER POSITION drills. Perform each set of jumps in rapid succession. Watch your form. Be sure you jump straight up and keep your skis a comfortable distance apart. When you land, compress your body to absorb the entire landing. Be sure you land straight and maintain your balance, all the way down.

Once you're able to jump and land repeatedly, all the while maintaining your balance, you'll begin to feel a natural, powerful, balanced stance. This stance is essential to learning to ski better because it means that your body is prepared to react to changing terrain and conditions.

Skiing in the Power Position

This short section is the bridge between understanding the Power Position and placing it in motion. There is no card and it is not on the video but is designed to help skiers integrate the Power Position into their skiing.

Many skiers enter the "Frozen Zone" at some point in a turn. The Frozen Zone is the point where the body loses the ability to be mobile. It has to do with being out of balance. Out of balance means out of alignment. Skiers need to constantly check alignment in order to stay balanced.

Good skiers are in constant motion; they never remain in any one position. For example, watch a pro mogul event or a ski race on TV. Notice that the skiers are always moving – up and down or side to side. These pro skiers are in smooth fluid motion and constantly adjust their balance to the changing terrain. They are skiing from the Power Position. Finding your Power Position will give you more control and confidence and free you from the Frozen Zone.

To find your Power Position, stand in an athletic position, feet shoulder-width apart, knees bent, and hands out in front holding ski poles. Now jump up and down twice, without planting your poles. Do this several times. Each time, try to be balanced and smooth. Try not to let the skis slap down upon landing. The secret is in moving from the body's center. Use the ball of the foot to take off and land on; absorb with the legs. Limit the movement of the arms and be certain not to bend at the waist.

The Power Position will be in between the first and second jump. From the time you land to the time you take off, the body is mobile, balanced, and in a constant state of motion. This is exactly how the great skiers ski. When the body is balanced and mobile, it can adjust to changes in terrain, speed, and position.

To put the Power Position into motion, find a spot on a trail below your ability where you feel safe skiing straight for 40 to 50 feet. The steepness of the trail plays no role in this drill, so play it safe and make sure the trail is not crowded. Ski straight down the trail and jump up and down three times; after the third jump, make a parallel stop. It is important to concentrate all the way through this drill. Most skiers fall trying to stop because they lighten up on their concentration. Repeat several times.

Keep in mind to be cat-like and anticipate your arrival back down on earth. This drill allows you to feel constant motion while moving down the mountain. It ensures that you remain in control by forcing you to stop. The stop is the beginning of applying the Power Position going into a turn.

Once you feel comfortable, replace the parallel stop with a turn to the left or right. After the turn, point the skis back down the hill. Jump up three times and turn in the other direction. Use a long traverse to keep your concentration and try not to stop your motion. Building confidence while moving is very important. Once this drill can be done at a consistent speed, progress is being made – so look for new terrain to conquer. The Power Position will allow skiers the freedom to become dynamic and adaptable.

Remember not spend too much time on one drill. Remain fresh and alert by taking breaks, then go free skiing to give the body a chance to practice what it has learned.

POWER POSITION TURN

The POWER POSITION TURN is a drill that forces skiers to be rhythmic, dynamic, balanced, and responsive. Note that this is a Green Circle drill if you have successfully mastered all of the drills previous to this one.

This drill is important for your ability to ski more challenging terrain. Clients who take the Extreme Team Advanced Ski clinics where I coach often ask me how can they prepare to ski more difficult terrain. I show them this drill and, if they can perform it and the three jumps in between two sets of turns, I tell them they are ready to take on new challenges.

Begin skiing straight down a gentle slope. Once you're in motion, jump up – just as you did in the previous drill. Remember what you learned about coming down and absorbing the jump. Don't tense up and stop the compression and absorption once your skis contact the snow. Stay loose and absorb the whole landing and spring up again.

> **Goal: To add downhill movement to the Power Position for a mobile, powerful stance**
>
> **Body Position: Ski straight downhill and jump up and down 3 times; then make 3 turns**

Perform three jumps, then cruise into a wide radius turn. Perform three turns, and then, if you're feeling comfortable, straighten out and perform three more jumps. Now, make three more turns.

51

As you follow the jumps with turns, you'll begin to feel a new power and confidence in the turns. Your skis will feel lighter on your feet and much more responsive. This is because you are skiing in a balanced mobile stance — nothing can get in your way.

This drill takes confidence and commitment. Make sure that your speed does not accelerate too much in the jumps. To control it, absorb the landing and use knee angulation and edge pressure in the turns to ski at a constant speed.

Mobility is the key term here. When we want to change direction or alter our skiing in some way, the most efficient way is by lifting our skis. Developing a powerful stance, along with the confidence and flexibility of the POWER POSITION, is an excellent way to increase our mobility. Practice this drill until you feel the power in the transitions between turning and jumping. With the new confidence in your ability to adjust and change your rhythm, you are skiing toward the Zone of Excellence.

POWER SLIDE

The first 14 drills in this book were designed to develop a proper balanced stance. The last two drills allowed you to add dynamic movement to a balanced stance. Now we are going to focus on developing awareness and on pressuring your skis.

Your skis are designed to do three things: sliding, edging, and carving. A sliding ski is a flat ski with no pressure or weight on the edges. An edged ski is a traversing ski. The ski is not turning but transporting the skier across the hill. A carving ski is a turning ski with pressure initiated to the shovel or front of the ski.

> **Goal: To feel a flat ski sliding in the fall line**
>
> **Body Position: Ski straight downhill; then pivot 90 degrees and slide down the fall line**

The POWER SLIDE drill focuses on a sliding ski with no pressure on its edges. This drill utilizes all of the body technique you have learned so far: shoulders square to the hill, hands out in front, head up, eyes looking down the hill. In this position, stand tall, perpendicular to the hill, while gravity pulls you down the hill.

The POWER SLIDE drill shows you how to use a flat ski in a highly controlled manner to slide sideways down the fall line – just by pivoting or twisting your lower body. The result is a higher awareness of your body's center, relative to a flat ski. You will be successful in this drill when you can slide down the hill in the fall line without any traverse or drifting off the fall line.

53

Begin skiing down a well-groomed slope with a fair amount of pitch to it. Stand up tall and ski straight, allowing yourself to pick up some speed. Square your shoulders to the hill and focus your gaze down the fall line.

Feel your feet. Concentrate on your feet as the center of the ski. Once you feel as perfectly balanced and centered as possible, pivot your body from the waist down and your skis 90 degrees to the left or right. Be sure you have pivoted only from the waist down, and that your upper body and your arms are facing downhill.

Once your skis have negotiated the pivot, turn your feet so that your skis are flat against the slope. Your legs, knees, and ankles need to be directly over your skis with no pressure or angulization. Do not use your edges! This will allow your skis to slide flat.

Check your center. Make sure your feet are equally weighted and hold the position comfortably. If you find yourself slowing down or drifting, you're using your edges. Flatten your skis by rolling your knees and ankles away from the hill. Your path is your result. If you are able to slide down the fall line, you are riding a flat ski. If your edges bite into the slope, then you will traverse or travel across the slope. Fine-tune your stance until you are sliding down the fall line. Notice in the video how Mihaela and I both slide directly down the fall line with no drifting left or right.

Take your time with this drill. It is important to feel your feet pivot the skis and then to feel the ski slide flat while across the fall line. The payoff will come by practicing and adjusting your stance. If your upper body is strong and calm and you are relaxed, then the pivot should be no problem. Finding the flat ski is a method of trying to adjust your lower body (legs, knees, ankles, and feet) against the slope.

Cut cards with scissors or knife along perforations. Do not rip cards from binding.
Card surfaces are weatherproof. For best protection place clear tape over card edges.

UPPER BODY – Downhill Hand Pressure
Dan Egan's Chairlift Guide to Skiing — 7

GOAL:
To illustrate how the downhill hand and arm translate pressure to your lower body.

BODY POSITION:
Around every turn, pretend someone is pulling on your downhill hand, trying to pull you down the hill.

As you initiate a turn, keep your downhill hand extended out past your downhill ski.

In the middle of the turn, your downhill shoulder should be over your downhill ski.

As you finish your turn and start to unweight, bring your hand slightly forward and keep it ahead of your body.

As you prepare for the next turn, make the new pole plant and exaggerate the pressure on the new downhill hand.

CARD 7A

POWER – Power Position
Dan Egan's Chairlift Guide to Skiing — 1

GOAL:
To define your Power Position as an athletic stance in constant fluid motion.

BODY POSITION:
Stand in an athletic position on a flat surface with skis on. Jump up and down three times.

Crouch down and jump up. Jump just high enough to get your skis off the ground.

Upon landing, absorb the impact by compressing all the way down.

Jump back up. Your power position starts when you spring up and ends after you absorb the landing.

Repeat three or four times. This teaches your body to naturally react to the situation. The result is a powerful, balanced stance.

CARD 8A

POWER – Power Slide
Dan Egan's Chairlift Guide to Skiing — 3

GOAL:
Feel a flat ski sliding in the fall line.

BODY POSITION:
Ski straight downhill, then pivot 90 degrees and slide down the fall line.

Stand tall and let your skis run straight. Keep your hands out in front, shoulders square to the hill.

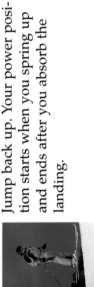

Pivot both skis 90 degrees, left or right. Make sure your feet are equally weighted. Pivot your body only from the waist down.

With your skis sideways, slide down the hill in a straight line. Don't pressure your edges.

The key to sliding straight is keeping your skis flat against the slope. A flat ski will slide down the fall line.

CARD 9A

Cut cards with scissors or knife along perforations. Do not rip cards from binding. Card surfaces are weatherproof. For best protection place clear tape over card edges.

POWER - Double Power Slide 4

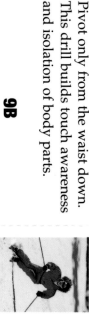

GOAL:
To master controlling a flat ski.

BODY POSITION:
Ski straight, power slide to one side, straighten out and power slide to the other side.

Stand tall and let your skis run straight. Keep your hands out in front, shoulders square to the hill.

Pivot both skis 90 degrees, left or right. Make sure your feet are equally weighted and pivot only from the waist down.

Straighten out your skis then perform a powerslide with skis pointing in the other direction.

Pivot only from the waist down. This drill builds touch awareness and isolation of body parts.

9B

POWER - Power Position Turn 2

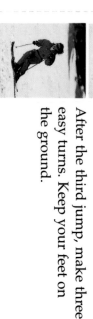

GOAL:
To add downhill movement to the Power Position for a mobile, powerful stance.

BODY POSITION:
Ski straight downhill and jump up and down three times then make three turns.

Glide downhill as you jump up and down three times. Absorb each landing to keep you fluid and loose.

After the third jump, make three easy turns. Keep your feet on the ground.

Let your skis straighten out, then jump up and down three more times.

Repeat three more turns. Feel the new power, balance and mobility.

8B

UPPER BODY - Downhill Hand Sweep 8

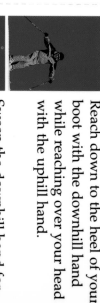

GOAL:
To illustrate how proper position of the upper body will completely control the lower body.

BODY POSITION:
Ski making large radius turns, sweeping your downhill hand past your boot.

Reach down to the heel of your boot with the downhill hand while reaching over your head with the uphill hand.

Sweep the downhill hand forward toward your toes.

Continue to sweep your downhill hand forward as you finish the turn and unweight by standing up.

Initiate the next turn by repeating this motion. The result is being able to make smooth, round turns.

7B

If you can't find your center, or if you seem to lose your awareness of centering, don't despair – just practice some more! Centering is what this drill emphasizes. Once you've sufficiently practiced, you'll find your lower body swiveling from your waist down like a hula dancer. The separation of upper and lower body plus the sensation of a flat ski are the benefits of this drill.

DOUBLE POWER SLIDE

Double your skills and double your fun with the DOUBLE POWER SLIDE drill! In this exercise, you'll learn to reverse the direction of slide from one side to the other. These skills help make it possible for you to ski the most difficult and extreme terrain. You are actually building a relationship with your skis by understanding how your body affects the position of the ski on the snow.

Practice this drill on the same slope where you performed the POWER SLIDE.

> Goal: To master controlling a flat ski
>
> Body Position: Ski straight; power slide to one side; straighten out and power slide to the other side

Begin skiing, just as you did before, straight down the hill, picking up a comfortable speed. Make sure your shoulders and head are facing downhill.

Now, find your center and pivot from the waist down, turning your skis just as you did before. Flatten your skis and power slide down the slope. Keep focused on your center, then straighten your skis out. Ski a short distance, then reverse the direction of the skis and continue to double power slide.

As you pivot your ski tips through the arc, remember to keep your skis flat against the snow. We are not using our edges to control or slow our descent in this drill. Instead, we are using an awareness of our body and its center and the ability to pivot from the waist down while keeping our upper body calm and relaxed in order to control our speed and movement.

The awareness you develop during the drill will take you into a whole new realm of skiing. When you can ride a flat ski directly down the fall line with the ability to change the direction of your skis without changing the direction of your body, you are truly experiencing power.

This skill is a prerequisite to entering what I call the Zone of Excellence. Continue practicing the DOUBLE POWER SLIDE until you don't have to check to see where your center is and until you can reverse direction with ease.

Remember, your path is your result. Study the video: The goal is to not drift or traverse across the hill. When you can double power slide in the fall line, you have mastered this drill.

POWER SLIDE TO TRAVERSE

Mastery of the flat ski is the prerequisite for mastering the ski's edge. That's because power comes from the ability to use a range of skills that can be applied to a ski. Not only will you derive more pleasure out of your skiing by knowing how to ski a flat ski and an edged ski, you will also gain control and confidence. Edge control is the second of the three foundation skills for ski control.

Goal: To feel the transition from a flat ski to a ski on edge

Body Position: ¾ of the way through a power slide, apply knee angulation and traverse the hill

Begin this drill by executing a power slide. As before, your upper body is relaxed, facing downhill, and your lower body is pivoted into the slide. Your knees and ankles are adjusted to ride a flat ski. Once you're ready to traverse, all you have to do is apply a little knee angulation. Roll your knees into the hill. As you do this, you are turning your downhill ski's edge into the snow, slowing your descent and causing your skis to traverse across the slope. This will bring you across the fall line.

The only difference between the POWER SLIDE and the POWER SLIDE TO TRAVERSE is knee angulation. Be sure you understand how it affects your centering and how much control you can achieve just by applying pressure to your edges. On the video, you will notice the difference between the POWER SLIDE drill and this one. You can clearly see Mihaela's knees rotate into the hill.

59

Practice this drill often and work carefully with it. As you become more proficient, you'll learn the right amount of touch necessary for selective edge pressuring.

Selective edge pressuring is the ability to apply pressure to your edges at different stages of a turn or descent. This is important in all-terrain skiing because it allows you the flexibility to touch your edges to the snow for control and to release your edges for control. This is a tool that you'll use again and again in mountain skiing. It will lead you further into the Zone of Excellence.

POWER SLIDE TO TURN

This drill is the third of the three foundation skills for ski control. The POWER SLIDE TO TRAVERSE added knee angulation to the POWER SLIDE. In order to allow you to make a turn, the POWER SLIDE TO TURN adds another subtle, but important, movement to the POWER SLIDE TO TRAVERSE.

Begin as you have before, skiing down the same slope. Keep your upper body calm, strong, and square to the slope. Be sure your arms are out in front of you and that you're looking downhill.

Go into a power slide, then apply knee angulation with forward pressure on your boots. Press your shins against the top of the boots. This downward pressure will initiate a carving and your skis will turn and angle back up the slope. Knee angulation causes pressure on the ski edge. Forward pressure on the boot puts pressure on the shovel of the ski. This simple illustration of a carved turn illustrates the difference between edging and

> **Goal: To teach the transition from a flat ski to a carving ski**
>
> **Body Position: Apply knee angulation and forward pressure to a power slide**

carving. Do this drill in both directions. As illustrated on the card and in the video, forward pressure and knee angulation can carve a ski with ease.

These three drills are the foundation for controlling your skis. The POWER SLIDE taught you to control a sliding ski. The POWER SLIDE TO TRAVERSE taught you to control the ski's edge. The POWER SLIDE TO TURN taught you control of a carving ski and combines the skills you learned in all three.

Practice these three foundation skills of sliding, edging, and carving until they are second nature. In the process, you will develop an innate sense of your center and a calm, strong upper body. Together, these skills and body knowledge will take you into the Zone of Excellence. By mastering these skills, you are becoming a more efficient skier, receiving the maximum return for the minimal amount of energy expenditure.

POWER TURN

The POWER SLIDE TO TRAVERSE drill applied the POWER POSITION to large radius turns. It's an excellent maneuver and can be used on all kinds of terrain and in all conditions. However, it works best only after you've mastered the three foundation skills. In the POWER TURN drill, you jump from a flat ski, land on a carving ski, and transition to an edged ski in the traverse, roll to a flat ski, and jump again into a new turn. The key to the POWER TURN is lift: You are going to get slightly airborne as you make turns!

> **Goal: To apply the Power Position turn to large radius turns**
>
> **Body Position: Make large radius turns and initiate each turn by jumping up and down the hill**

Begin skiing down an intermediate slope that has some challenge for you. As you are preparing to make a turn or change direction, jump up. Your body should be facing down the fall line, which will keep you perpendicular to the slope. The idea is to jump at the moment you begin the turn and, as you become airborne, let your skis follow and land in a turn. Watch the illustration in the video closely to see the uphill and downhill motion. Notice how your feet follow your hips.

Use your downhill pole to leverage your jump. Land in a turn with your body once again perpendicular to the hill, your skis pointing slightly across the slope, your hands and poles out in front of your body. Remember to absorb the landing by bending your knees and crouching down. You should feel the pressure in the front of your boots upon landing, which will help you carve your way through the turn. Complete the traverse and begin another turn in the opposite direction, then perform the POWER TURN once more.

As you practice, strive to achieve the most perfect poise and balance you can. Strive for a constant, fluid motion; think of the jumps and turns as a continuous process, not as discrete, independent steps. As you feel more comfortable with the POWER TURN, try linking three or four of them together. This will enhance the feeling of continuous motion.

As you master the POWER TURN, you will feel an increased confidence to ski on unfamiliar terrain. The jumping will increase your power and mobility, and you'll find yourself seeking new challenges and things to ski over, under, and around. Go for it!

JACKRABBIT TURN

The JACKRABBIT TURN drill builds strength and dynamic motion. It calls on your coordination and uses the POWER POSITION to generate the motion. This drill is important because doing it builds confidence as you learn how to pick your feet up in a short radius turn and set them down in a new direction. Be sure you're warmed up and full of energy for this drill; it requires a lot of hard work and stamina!

Goal: To build quickness, independent leg action, and powerful short radius turns

Body Position: Ski downhill making jump turns

The JACKRABBIT TURN is the POWER TURN with attitude: Instead of a jump, it's an energetic leap combined with lateral movement and a powerful pole plant. It's a skill that builds quick reactions and teaches independent leg action. The JACKRABBIT TURN teaches you to pick up your feet and create powerful short radius turns. Being able to jump into the air and come down in a new turn is a skill often used on particularly steep or challenging runs, and it ultimately sets the serious skier apart from the casual one.

In practice, the JACKRABBIT TURN is easy to learn and practice. It's as simple as – well, jumping! Just pick your feet up together and place them in a new direction. In fact, you may want to practice it without skis on to build strength and confidence, similar to the JUMP TURNS WITHOUT SKIS drill in the Balance section.

As shown on the video, you can practice this drill in your living room.

On the slope, face downhill and push off. Be sure your body is in proper balance and well-centered. Once you're in motion, crouch down, then leap into the air. An essential characteristic of the JACKRABBIT TURN is this explosive upward movement. Place your feet down in the new direction. Be sure to turn your skis in the air. Land and jump up again and make another turn. Use your pole plant. For leverage, timing, and balance, independent leg action will help you move laterally across the snow because you can initiate the upward motion of the jump with your uphill leg.

Practice this drill in sets. Do as many JACKRABBIT TURNS as you can, then take a rest and do another set. As you continue to practice, you'll see yourself becoming stronger, quicker, and a much more powerful and proactive skier. You'll experience dramatic improvements in your slalom turns, steep skiing, and tree skiing.

Time Out

Let's take a moment to review the key points of what we have learned so far.

Balance. In the first section, Balance, we learned about the efficient use of our body in relation to gravity. The Balance section also illustrated the use of knee and hip angulation as well as foot placement.

Upper Body. The Upper Body section taught upper body positioning. The concept of isolation and separation of body parts was introduced to create a relationship between all body parts while in constant fluid motion. We learned where to focus our eyes as well as proper the hand and arm position for pole plants.

Power. Next, Power was introduced. We learned that a powerful stance is one that is never stagnant or rigid. Drills in this section illustrated how power can be fluid and graceful as well as explosive and dynamic. We also learned the three foundation skills for ski control: sliding, edging, and carving.

Fluidity and Agility. In the next two sections, Fluidity and Agility, the drills take the skier through a range of skills that build upon the concepts you have learned. Pay attention to every drill as each plays a part in working toward your improved ability in all-terrain skiing.

The goal now is to add the elements of greater body awareness through isolation and separation of body parts, constant fluid motion for greater ski control, and the ability to adapt to changing terrain, conditions, speed, and situations.

As you move ahead, internalize the motions and visualize the action of the carving ski. Try to imagine what it feels like to have your body and skis accomplishing the goal of efficient movements for greater skiing control, power, fluidity, and agility.

If you start to have problems with any of the drills, review different sections to identify your problem areas. Identify the part of the body that is causing you to lose your balance or lose control of your skis. Then think about which drills you had trouble with; there you will probably find the correlation of past and present problems.

It's time to move on to the last two sections. If, at any point, a drill stumps you or you hit a roadblock, review the previous sections, the cards, or the video.

Fluidity

Fluidity adds the art of dance to the movement of skiing. This is the point where you will discover how to overcome and break through to new levels of ability.

By this point, you are getting really tuned in to your body position; you have the tools and you are learning how to use them. Your free skiing is improving and you are anticipating changes in conditions and terrain. Speed is no longer an element that scares you; rather, you can control it and enjoy it a little more. All this has been accomplished through understanding your body position and its effects on your skis.

Now it's time to add fluidity, grace, and rhythm. It's time to complement the hill with your skiing presence. In this section, you will learn how to ski the mountain without letting it ski you.

I define fluidity in skiing as the ability to readjust body position through minor adjustments in order to stay in control. Situation skiing is the best way to allow skiers to find the dance within themselves. The result will be a more fluid style of skiing.

The drills in this section are designed for the skier to accomplish a task or get into a body position not achieved before. The goal is to illustrate how positioning your body or skis will allow you to change direction and turn. The first drill, KNEE ROLL, focuses on knee angulation and how it carves a ski. LEAD THE SKI illustrates how ski positioning can carve a ski. The

FUNNY WALK drill combines the previous two drills and forces the skier to use knee angulation and ski positioning with dynamic independent leg action, resulting in direct edge pressure to the snow.

The FUNNY WALK TURN adds fluid motion to direct edge pressure and will help skiers internalize the feeling of fluid turning skis. These four drills are all combined in the WEDGE TO RACE drill which allows skiers to identify the similarities between a snowplow turn and a race turn.

FUN AND GAMES is a drill combining total body movement with knee angulation, pole planting, and edge control. This drill prepares you for the TURNS WITHIN A TURN drill that places skiers into a situation of selective edge pressuring and will build what I call "the touch." The touch will be needed for the JAVELIN TURN drill. This drill builds confidence in the skills learned in this section. Accomplishing javelin turns is a sign of progress and fluidity.

Egan Entertainment Network
800-619-6801

INSTRUCTIONAL PRODUCTS

A. Chairlift Ski Guide - From novice to expert, Dan Egan, Extreme Skier and his wife Mihaela, a three-time Romanian Olympic Skier, teach you the fundamentals of proper ski techniques. This coordinated guide includes a book (ALL TERRAIN SKIING), Training Video (complete with exercises) and 19 cards you can select drills from for your ride up the mountain.
Complete Set - $49.95
Book/Instruction Cards - $24.95
Video - $29.95

B. Advance To The Steeps - $29.95
Featuring Dan and John Egan, Rob and Eric DesLauriers and Dean Decas. Learn the secrets from the best all-terrain skiers in the world.

ACTION VIDEOS

C. The Extreme Dream: Price - $14.95
D. Return of the Shred-I: Price - $19.95
E Where The Steeps Have No Name - $19.95

KIDS VIDEOS

F. Children of the Snow: Price - $14.95

Order now by calling **1-(800) 619-6801**

Shipping and Handling Charges -
Merchandise Total	Add Shipping and Handling
$10.00 to $25.00	$3.50 per order
$26.00 and up	$5.00 per order

Allow 3 to 4 weeks for delivery.
American Express, Mastercard and Visa accepted.

Dan Egan's Chairlift Guide to Skiing
POWER – The Power Turn
7

GOAL:
The goal of this drill is to apply the Power Position turn to large radius turns.

BODY POSITION:
Make large radius turns and initiate each turn by jumping up and down the hill.

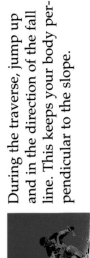

During the traverse, jump up and in the direction of the fall line. This keeps your body perpendicular to the slope.

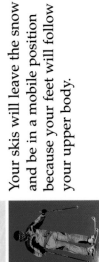

Your skis will leave the snow and be in a mobile position because your feet will follow your upper body.

Land in a turn with your upper body square to the hill and your hands out in front.

Absorb the landing by bending your knees and pressuring the front of your boots. Repeat the drill.

CARD 11A

Dan Egan's Chairlift Guide to Skiing
POWER – Power Slide to Traverse
5

GOAL:
To feel the transition from a flat ski to a ski on edge.

BODY POSITION:
3/4 of the way through a power slide apply knee angulation and traverse the hill.

Stand tall and let your skis run straight. Keep your hands out in front, shoulders square to the hill.

Pivot both skis 90 degrees, left or right. Make sure your feet are equally weighted and pivot only from the waist down.

Apply knee angulation and traverse across the hill.

This drill teaches the difference between a sliding (flat) ski and an edged ski. The difference is knee angulation.

CARD 10A

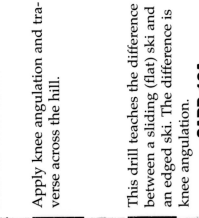

Cut cards with scissors or knife along perforations. Do not rip cards from binding.
Card surfaces are weatherproof. For best protection place clear tape over card edges.

Egan Entertainment Network
800-619-6801

For Information on the Extreme Team
Advanced Ski Clinics:
1-800-X-TEAM-70

Locations across North America and around the world.

A

E

F

C

D

Dan Egan's Chairlift Guide to Skiing
POWER – Jackrabbit Turn
◆ 8

GOAL:
The goal of this drill is to build quickness, independent leg action, and powerful short radius turns.

BODY POSITION:
Ski downhill making jump turns.

Ski forward. Crouch down, then jump up.

Lift both feet off the ground.

Use your pole to generate lateral movement.

Land in a new turn and repeat. This skill will allow you to ski nearly any terrain.

11B

Dan Egan's Chairlift Guide to Skiing
POWER – Power Slide to Turn
6

GOAL:
The goal of this drill is to teach the transition from a flat ski to a carving ski.

BODY POSITION:
Apply knee angulation and forward pressure to a power slide.

Stand tall and let your skis run straight. Keep your hands out in front, shoulders square to the hill.

Pivot both skis 90 degrees, left or right. Make sure your feet are equally weighted and pivot only from the waist down.

Apply knee angulation simultaneously with forward pressure. Carve a turn slightly up the hill.

Finish the turn by unweighting and releasing the knee angulation. Repeat in both directions.

10B

KNEE ROLL

When you first learned the snowplow turn, nobody told you that you were making the perfect race turn. Well, I'm telling you now. I'll illustrate that point with further clarification of a carved turn and you'll see how easily a snowplow turn can become a race turn. But first, we go back to basics and practice the KNEE ROLL. We are now into the fine-tuning aspects of skiing. This means we have to isolate body parts and feel the effect on our performance.

Goal: To teach knee angulation

Body Position: Start in a snowplow with your hands on the outside of your knees

The KNEE ROLL drill is one of my favorites. From beginners to experts, this drill reinforces edge control through knee angulation. It also allows skiers to internalize the feeling of a carving ski. The remark I hear most from skiers is that they finally realize how little effort it takes to turn a ski.

Start out on a moderate slope. Facing downhill, form a wedge with your skis or a snowplow stop. Stand still. Now place your hands on the outside of your knees. Release the edge pressure of your wedge and start to glide forward.

Put some pressure against the right or left knee, pressing it in toward your other knee. At the same time, put some pressure on the front of your boot. You will feel yourself beginning to carve a turn. You will notice that your knees are touching, with the downhill knee angulated and pressured. This is the A-FRAME.

71

As you continue applying pressure against your knee and toes, you will continue to turn. Notice how easy it is to control your movement with so little physical exertion!

Now, release the pressure and you'll feel yourself ending the turn. Let yourself traverse for a short distance, then repeat the pressure using the other leg. Don't use your feet or ski tips to initiate the turn. Let the pressure of knee angulation do it for you.

Continue to repeat this drill a few more times. As you do so, notice what happens to the edge of your ski. The knee angulation pressure is turning your ski up on its edge to carve the turn. When your ski is on edge, it is important not to push or twist your foot. Feel how easy it is to do when you use the KNEE ROLL.

Remember, pressure the knee, don't twist the foot. And notice that it only takes a gentle pressure to carve a turn. Our goal is to expend the minimal amount of energy to achieve the maximum result. That way, we get to ski better for longer periods of time!

Knee angulation allows skiers to make quick, rapid turns. It also expands the range of control for situation skiing like moguls, trees, and steeps.

LEAD THE SKI

Now that we are on the path of fluidity, we will stop once again to study how to expend minimal energy to achieve maximum results. The LEAD THE SKI drill is another illustration of how effortless skiing can be.

The LEAD THE SKI drill teaches us the importance of a well-balanced mobile stance in relation to our feet. This drill calls for the ability to shuffle our feet slightly in order to achieve efficient movement while turning.

Begin skiing in a gentle snowplow. Look at the tips of your skis as you begin to move. As you start to descend, move the uphill ski tip out in front of the

> Goal: To illustrate how our skis are an extension of our feet
>
> Body Position: As you ski across the hill, push your uphill ski tip out in front of the downhill ski tip to initiate a turn

downhill ski. This becomes your lead ski, because it is going to lead you into the turn. Now apply knee angulation and forward pressure to your boot. Notice that you are beginning to turn in the direction of the lead ski. That's exactly what's supposed to occur. Don't let your lead ski get too far out in front, though; it should not extend past the trailing ski more than the tip's to half the shovel's length.

As you let your lead ski make the turn for you, notice that something else is happening: your hips are naturally becoming square to the hill. This keeps your body in proper position throughout the turn. It also means that all the turning motion is originating in your hips, where your body is strong. This occurs

73

because your lead ski is turning toward the fall line as opposed to trying to turn by twisting your feet and ankles.

As you complete the turn, your ski tips will realign themselves together. Stay in the snowplow position and let the formerly trailing ski push out in front to become the lead ski. Now feel yourself begin to negotiate another turn and remember to apply knee angulation for forward pressure to your boot. The turning should feel effortless.

Effortless and efficient. Achieving maximum response or movement with minimal energy expenditure. That is achieving fluidity. Stop and think about past situations when you could not turn in time or when you wanted to turn and the result was less than perfect. Now visualize yourself skiing more advanced terrain with fluidity and control, making subtle movements and turning where you please. This simple drill will take you to new heights and a new level of awareness. Your body and equipment are forming a relationship, a bond, and the result is a more fluid style of skiing.

FUNNY WALK

It's funny, but a lot of people think the snowplow position is only for beginning skiers. The truth is, the A-FRAME position – forming an A with your legs or your knees – is a very powerful position that gives you a lot of direct edge pressure. As our ability increases, we gain range in when to apply pressure to our edges and, thus, the more fluid we become. The knee roll in LEAD THE SKI taught us a gentle, light touch to our edges. The FUNNY WALK teaches direct edge pressure. Direct edge pressure allows skiers instant control because the ski is forced to perform on demand.

We're going to exaggerate the A-FRAME position to practice a drill called the FUNNY WALK. An experienced skier watching you perform the FUNNY WALK will immediately recognize the impact of the drill. You too can check your progress when the drill is completed by studying the marks left behind on the snow. All that is left on the snow will be impressions of your edges, no sliding or skid marks. The benefits of this drill will be felt in slalom skiing, mogul skiing, and on hard-packed snow.

Goal: To illustrate the importance of applying instant edge pressure

Body Position: Ski down the hill with your knees in an A-FRAME and alternate stepping on your inside edges

Begin this drill by standing in a snowplow facing downhill with your knees in an A-FRAME. This will bring you up on the inside edges of your skis. Now, start to move forward. Walk like a duck, touching only

75

the inside edges to the snow. Take short, quick steps, moving straight down the hill – don't make any turns. Your speed should help you keep a lively pace. Be sure you're only using your ski edges. If you start to go too fast, dig your edges into the snow with more force as you set them down. Watch the video to see how a ski with direct edge pressure does not skid.

Keep those knees together! Lift your feet one at a time, touch and release, touch and release. This drill helps you develop edge control by shifting from ski to ski while maintaining contact with the snow. After ten steps, stop and look back at the hill. You should notice edge marks only alternating down the hill. If you felt your skis sliding or see skid marks, you need more knee angulation. Check your A-FRAME. As you repeat this drill, make sure to place only the inside edge on the snow, not the base of the ski.

This drill allows skiers to realize that they can place a ski on edge and instantly get results. Direct edge pressure forces your skis to react and perform.

FUNNY WALK TURN

The FUNNY WALK TURN is an extension of the FUNNY WALK. Eric DesLauriers calls this drill the Drunken Sailor. It paints the picture of someone bobbing and weaving their way down the street. Well, we want to bob and weave our way down the slope in a relaxed, fluid manner. This drill, when done correctly, ties together all of the drills in this section and takes us along the path of fluidity.

In the FUNNY WALK TURN, we learn how to get more out of the FUNNY WALK. We're going to use the same stepping motions but will keep our skis in contact with the snow for a longer period. We'll use knee angulation and direct edge pressure to gain more fluidity. The result is the ability to make very fluid ski turns.

Stand in a snowplow with your knees in the A-FRAME. Start to walk like a duck but this time leave your ski on the snow a little longer. The result will be a turning ski, because of the direct edge pressure and an angulated ski. The ski should turn upon snow contact. As you start to get the feel of this drill, you will realize that the turning ski turns under your body or, in other words, as you step from edge to edge and as you release the direct edge pressure, your foot should be under your body as you instantly step onto the new edge. Do this drill several

> **Goal: To enhance your fluidity through knee angulation and edge pressure**
>
> **Body Position: Perform a FUNNY WALK but allow more time for each ski on the snow**

77

times. Develop a feeling and sense of timing. To help visualize this, watch the video to burn the image into your mind.

Let's review the action of this drill. Start skiing in a wedge with knees in an A-FRAME. Now walk like a duck touching only the inside edges to the snow, one at a time. As the inside edge of a ski touches the snow, pause and let the ski react to the direct edge pressure. The result will be a ski that turns. As you get more fluid, the ski will move under your body because, as you release the direct edge pressure and step to the other ski, the first ski will finish its turn. Further along in the Agility section, you will see how this will help you in mogul skiing.

The FUNNY WALK TURN will give you a greater feeling of fluidity. Practice it as much as possible; in time you will begin to internalize these motions and they will become an integral part of your skiing. No longer will you feel you need to have both skis firmly planted on the snow in order to turn or change direction. The FUNNY WALK TURN is another milestone on the trail to the Zone of Excellence.

WEDGE TO RACE

Fluidity will allow you to progress from one style of skiing to another. The WEDGE TO RACE drill requires you to start in a snowplow turn and progress to a race turn. As you attempt this drill, remember to feel your downhill ski carve through every turn.

Start skiing and turning in a wedge. Use knee angulation and make a few turns to warm up. Keep your upper body still and exert pressure at the front of your boot. Remember the KNEE ROLL and LEAD THE SKI drills. As you progress to the third and fourth turn, make your wedge smaller each time by unweighting your uphill ski while bringing your skis more closely together.

Goal: To illustrate the similarities between a snowplow turn and a race turn

Body Position: Start in a wedge turn and transform into a parallel turn

Continue making turns, bringing your skis parallel. Now you have completed the transition from a wedge turn to a race turn. Practice doing this with grace and fluidity. You can now see how easy it is to make a good race carved turn and how each step is related.

This drill shows how knee angulation, edge pressure, and independent leg action are used in all types of turns. With each turn you'll gain the confidence and the skills to ski the mountain with ease, grace, and control. The more fluid you become, the easier it is to go from wedge to race. On the path to fluidity, you are getting closer to the Zone of Excellence.

FUN AND GAMES

Fluidity isn't just smooth skiing; it's also being able to react quickly. That's where fun and games come in. The FUN AND GAMES drill tests your reactions, works on balance, shows you how to achieve fluid motion through the isolation and separation of body parts, and is a great energy drill as well!

The purpose of this drill is to orchestrate the body in unison. FUN AND GAMES spans the entire gamut of body dynamics. In this drill, you will work with your poles, shoulders, arms, hands, hips, legs, knees, edges and boots, and feet.

Begin by facing down the hill, head up, body square, and eyes looking down the fall line. Push off and quickly perform three medium radius turns, using knee angulation to do so. On the third turn, come to a quick stop by setting your edges and immediately take three steps up the slope. On the third step, swing your ski tips downhill and push off again. Repeat the three turns; stop in the other direction, and take three short, slow steps uphill (but build to a quicker pace) to increase your strength and reaction time.

> **Goal:** To reinforce the importance of a powerful, balanced stance through separation and isolation of body parts
>
> **Body Position:** Ski medium radius turns; stop and take 3 steps up the hill and then ski again

Taking steps back uphill teaches the isolation and separation of body parts, specifically the arms and

81

feet. It also demonstrates how the entire body must work as a whole in all-terrain skiing. This drill illustrates how, through a simple task of sidestepping up the hill, natural body positioning replaces technical knowledge.

This is a great drill to do mid-morning when your energy level is high. It demands total body and equipment synergy. The fluidity comes from coordination and the relationship between body, equipment, and mountain.

Turns Within a Turn

By now, you've become more aware of how to pressure your skis and boots. You know how to make several different types of turns and you know how to use your skis to control your movement and direction. The goal of this drill is to further prepare you for the unanticipated eventuality of obstacles and conditions. This is where the Turns Within a Turn drill comes into play.

This drill helps you learn how to make those mid-turn changes that always come up when you least expect them – like when you're carving a beautiful slalom turn and the snow goes from soft to hard or somebody comes skiing right across your path. Similar to the Power Slide drills, you will build selective edge pressure instead of constant direct pressure.

Goal: To teach selective edge pressuring

Body Position: In between medium radius turns, pressure the uphill ski twice on the traverse as if you were going to make a turn; complete the turn only on the second attempt

Begin skiing on an intermediate slope, making medium radius turns. Once you're comfortable and relaxed, start a new turn – but don't finish it. That skier is skiing right for you! Notice that you have applied pressure to the uphill ski. To cancel the turn, release the pressure on the uphill ski and resume skiing in the original direction on the downhill ski. Now, initiate the turn once again with the uphill ski. Begin to roll your knee in and feel the ski begin to turn. If the skier is still in your path, let up once more. Continue your traverse, then initiate the turn once again and complete it.

Practice this drill in both directions until you feel yourself becoming fluid and graceful in your turns within a turn. This drill is great for becoming mobile and versatile. Skiers who can touch and release edge pressure can ski a variety of terrain, avoid obstacles, and adapt to changing conditions.

Stay with this drill and practice it. Become confident to the point where, during your traverse, you can change the number of times you turn within a turn. On one traverse, initiate two turns; on the next, do three or one. Changing your rhythm will increase your skill level. You will feel a new awareness of your ability developing inside you.

I call this "the touch." It feels great, doesn't it?

JAVELIN TURN

The purpose of the JAVELIN TURN is to help you develop your hip angulation and gain more confidence and stability in long radius turns. This is a Black Diamond drill because you have to balance on the uphill ski and keep your upper body calm and strong while rolling your hip and turning the ski. The key to this is *trust.* Trust that by having proper body position, you can create the end result. And also, trust the new feeling that your balance and stance will stay intact while skiing on one ski.

On an intermediate slope, begin a long traverse. Now, stand on your uphill ski and raise your downhill ski off the snow. Just so you won't be tempted to put it back down, cross the downhill ski tip over your uphill ski. Once in this position, roll your hips down the fall line. Keep your shoulders and hand facing down the hill. Don't tilt or lean your shoulders into the hill. Instead, angulate from the hip so that your feet move out away from your body. Refer to Card 3A, Drill 5, the FOOT PLACEMENT drill. Once the turn is complete, uncross your skis and step up onto the new uphill ski and begin the JAVELIN TURN once more. If you're at all confused about this drill, watch the video for the sequence of body movements.

> **Goal: To reinforce hip angulation and stability at high speeds**
>
> **Body Position: Make large radius turns; initiate each turn on the uphill ski with the downhill ski off the snow**

The ability to shift your weight and control, using hip angulation, is a major benefit of the JAVELIN TURN. It is very useful when making giant slalom turns. As you become proficient with the JAVELIN TURN, you'll find that you're able to ski in a very stable stance and at high speeds.

All of this sounds harder than it is. When you break this drill down, the elements are simple and happen simultaneously.

- Step onto the uphill ski.
- Lift the downhill ski off the snow and cross it over the uphill ski.
- Roll hips down the fall line, which will turn you across the hill.
- Repeat.

Rolling your hips down the fall line creates the hip angulation which pressures and edges the ski; stepping up to the new uphill ski unweights and finishes the turn as you initiate a new one. Once you get this motion, you will find a stable hip position which will allow you to ski faster. This drill is similar to the POWER TURN drill in that it builds large stable radius turns. You've got nothing to lose...go for it!

Cut cards with scissors or knife along perforations. Do not rip cards from binding. Card surfaces are weatherproof. For best protection place clear tape over card edges.

FLUIDITY - Wedge to Race

GOAL:
To illustrate the similarities between a snowplow turn and a race turn.

BODY POSITION:
Start in a wedge turn and transform into a parallel turn.

Make two wedge turns using knee angulation.

On turns three and four, make less of a wedge and start to slide your skis closer together.

As your skis become parallel, continue to pressure the front of your boots to initiate turns.

Continue making race turns using knee angulation and forward pressure to initiate each turn.

CARD 14A

FLUIDITY - Funny Walk

GOAL:
To illustrate the importance of applying instant edge pressure.

BODY POSITION:
Ski down hill with your knees in an A-Frame, and alternate stepping on your inside edges.

Stay in the A-FRAME and start to ski by lifting one ski off the ground.

As you begin to glide, take quick short steps but remain in an A-FRAME.

Only the inside edges of your skis should touch the snow.

This independent leg action and instant edge-to-snow contact will make you quicker going from edge to edge.

CARD 13A

FLUIDITY - Knee Roll

GOAL:
To teach knee angulation.

BODY POSITION:
Start in a snowplow with your hands on the outside of your knees.

Begin skiing with your hands on the outside of your knees but not applying pressure.

To initiate a turn, push one knee toward the other to create an A-FRAME.

Maintain pressure against the knee throughout the whole turn.

Release the knee and initiate the new turn by pressing against the opposite knee.

CARD 12A

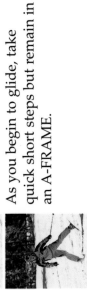
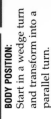

Cut cards with scissors or knife along perforations. Do not rip cards from binding. Card surfaces are weatherproof. For best protection place clear tape over card edges.

GOAL:
To reinforce the importance of a powerful, balanced stance through separation and isolation of body parts.

BODY POSITION:
Ski medium radius turns. Stop and take three steps up the hill, then ski again.

Make three medium radius turns with knee angulation.

Stop after the third turn and take three quick steps back up the hill.

After the third turn, push off and make three more turns.

Taking three steps up the hill demands that your whole body works as a unit.

14B

GOAL:
To enhance your fluidity through knee angulation and edge pressure.

BODY POSITION:
Perform a Funny Walk but allow more time for each ski on the snow.

Stay in the A-FRAME and ski by lifting one ski off the ground and applying pressure to the front of your boot.

Leave the ski on the snow longer than you did in the Funny Walk.

Step between skis and feel each ski turn and come under your body.

This is a fluid movement. Your skis should be turning the instant they hit the snow.

13B

GOAL:
To illustrate how our skis are an extension of our feet.

BODY POSITION:
Skiing in a wedge, making medium radius turns.

To initiate a turn, push the uphill ski tip slightly ahead of the downhill ski tip.

Pressure the edge of the lead ski with knee angulation.

Transition between turns by pushing the new uphill ski tip in front of the new downhill ski.

Turning should be effortless, pushing your tip forward and squaring your hips to the hill for proper positioning.

12B

Agility

Cards 16 through 19

Agility is the result of a developed sense of movement. An agile skier cannot only go wherever he or she pleases, but gets there with grace. An agile skier flows so beautifully that his or her body floats above the snow, always seeking the path of least resistance.

Since fluidity adds the art of dance to skiing movement, agility allows skiers to dance on any part of the mountain they choose, in any conditions. The goal is to operate in the Zone of Excellence.

Joseph Campbell once said that the best things in life cannot be expressed in words, the second-best things in life are the ones we think about, and the third-best things in life are the ones we talk about. In other words, the ultimate ski run has no translation from experience to words. My friend Peter Gardiner once described the smile on my face in a skiing photograph as sublime.

For example, in 1991 I was skiing in what was then Yugoslavia; today this section of the world is called Slovenia. The ski area we started from is called Kanine, a beautiful small ski area on the Italian border. The summit station is surrounded by mountain peaks that extend another 1,500 to 2,000 feet up. Their slopes are steep and covered with a combination of cliffs, narrow shoots, and wide open faces. A perfect place to ski.

The problem was that our descent was different from our climb up. We were sure of the snow conditions but unsure of our way through the rocks below. Our cameraman, Tom Day, set up across the valley and, communicating via radio, yelled "Camera rolling!" In the excitement and anticipation of my first turn, I dropped one of my ski poles and it tumbled down the steep face and out of sight.

Without hesitation, I jumped in and started skiing the 50-degree face with one pole. After that, my memory is vague. I remember lots of moving snow following my every turn; I remember entering the cliff band with a constant speed and with belief in my ability; then I remember seeing a way through the rocks and off a cliff. The landing and the turns afterwards to the bottom were nothing but a sense of freedom, power, and my internal smile.

Months later, when I saw the film, it was an out-of-body experience for me. I remembered being there and I knew I had skied it, but I noticed so many details that I had not been able to recall. That's when I realized that when you are operating in the Zone of Excellence, mind and body act as one with instinctive reactions that allow you to perform extraordinary feats.

The discussion, drills, and skills learned in this final section of the book center around developing an instinctive reaction with yourself. The THOUSAND STEP drill will identify your frozen zone; the THREE-STEP TURN will develop instinctive reaction time. The THREE-STEP OUTSIDE TURN *forces* skiers to rely on instinctive reaction time. It is the toughest drill in the book. ONE-LEGGED SKIING will incorporate the previous two drills into one.

The MOGUL WALK, MIND OVER MOGUL, and MOGUL RIDE help skiers find the path of least resistance. The NON-STOP SKIING drill ties the whole package together and allows skiers the time and freedom to experience the Zone of Excellence.

THOUSAND STEPS

Small steps lead to big leaps in your skiing improvement. That's the reason for all these drills. In the THOUSAND STEPS drill, the small steps are designed to help you identify your "frozen zone." Your frozen zone is the exact moment when you know you are out of balance and unable to move your feet. It's when we feel locked, stiff, and unable to react. Usually the result is a skidding ski or upper body rotation.

This drill will help you identify your frozen zone and teach you the mobility, independent leg action, and agility necessary to overcome it. Taking lots of small steps will help you in a big way.

Goal: To establish agile, independent leg action

Body Position: Make large radius downhill turns and keep your legs walking throughout the whole run

Begin by traversing across the hill – but walk, do not ski. Take many small, light steps with your skis. You should never have both skis on the ground at the same time. Keep your upper body still and square with the slope. As you approach the point where you must begin to turn and reverse direction, continue to make small steps. You may want to put both feet down, but don't do it! Continue stepping through the turn.

Your frozen zone will be identified at the point where you are unable to continue to step. At that point, your body is out of alignment and your agility, fluidity, and power are all lost. Remember that you should be floating down the hill. Be relaxed; take small light steps. Most skiers have problems in the belly of the turn. If this is true for you, then review some drills like FOOT PLACEMENT, POWER POSITION TURN, LEAD THE SKI, or JAVELIN TURN. These drills all deal with proper body position in relation to your feet.

This drill calls for isolation and separation of body parts, constant fluid motion, and eyes looking down the hill. Keep your hands where you can see them, upper body calm and strong, and focus on hip angulation rather than knee angulation.

Unlocking your frozen zone(s) and performing multiple tasks with your body while skiing is agility. Practice this drill until you can step through large and small radius turns. This skill will allow you to become agile in moguls, crud, and hard-pack. It's a great way to launch yourself into all-terrain skiing.

Continue this drill all the way down the mountain. After you've practiced it for a while, you will begin to feel an increase in your agility. This is because you have unlocked your lower body. Even when you don't realize it, you can be out of balance, which will create a frozen zone. This drill will set you free.

THREE-STEP TURN

Agile skiers have the skill to change rhythm and direction while skiing at a constant speed. The THREE-STEP TURN drill requires both these skills. The challenge of this drill is for skiers to keep their composure and stay focused on the task. Remember, thinking slows down reaction time; visualization and trusting your instinct increase reaction time. By this point in the book, it is critical that you believe you can acquire these skills.

The THREE-STEP TURN drill is as follows: Ski down a gentle slope and lift one ski off the snow as if you are marching, just as in the SKI WALKING drill. Do this three times (three steps). After the third step, make three slalom turns in the fall line. After the third turn, take three more steps and then make three more turns.

This drill requires you to handle acceleration, dynamic motion, isolation and separation of body parts, and knee angulation for edge pressure. Don't forget all that you learned in the FUNNY WALK TURN drill. Keep all of your momentum going down the fall line with a calm and strong upper body and fluid agile lower body.

> **Goal: To enhance reaction time through change in rhythm**
>
> **Body Position: Make 3 moving marching steps; then make 3 turns**

Repeat until there is no hesitation between the marching steps and the first turn plus no hesitation between the last turn and the next marching step. If you are having trouble containing your speed, use the

91

turns to regain control. Do this by using more knee angulation and forward pressure to create more edging and a sharper turn.

The THREE-STEP TURN is the foundation for the next four drills, so spend some time mastering this one. Watch the video to get a sense of timing and control. Notice that our body position does not change between the steps and the turns: The body mechanics remain the same. Let your mind relax and your body take over. A balanced mobile stance with a calm and strong upper body results in a powerful, fluid, and agile turn.

THREE-STEP OUTSIDE TURN

You have reached the last major hurdle in this book. There is a saying that goes "When the going gets tough, the tough go pro." Well, it's all Black Diamond drills from here to the end. Put a lot of energy into this one, because it teaches visualization and rapid reaction time – two really critical skills if you want to be an all-terrain skier skiing in the Zone of Excellence.

The major difference between this drill and the THREE-STEP TURN is that the three turns in this drill are performed with the uphill ski on the outside edge. That's right — uphill ski, outside edge. The trick is to keep your skis turning in the fall line and not allow them to slide or skid across the hill. Roll your hip into the slope in order to turn the uphill ski on the outside edge.

> **Goal: To trust your reaction time**
>
> **Body Position: Make 3 moving marching steps; then 3 turns on the outside edge of the uphill ski**

If it sounds hard, you're right. Study the video and pay attention to the illustrations. The key is in the hips. Let's try it. Same intermediate slope as before, three marching steps. As you finish your third step, slightly roll your hip into the hill. Don't lean it, just roll your hip. This will create hip angulation on the uphill ski and you will turn. Keep your upper body calm and strong as always. Release the hip angulation by stepping back onto the other ski and roll up onto the new uphill ski's outside edge. Once again, for the third turn, step down onto the other ski and roll your hip into the hill.

This is primarily a mental drill. Make sure you clear your mind of any preconceptions about how to ski. Here is something new you need to experience on the path to the Zone of Excellence.

Don't try to make big or sharp turns on the uphill ski. Just give it a touch of hip angulation – it will turn. Be relaxed and stay forward in your boots. Try to control your speed and flow with the action. This drill takes confidence and a couple of tries to get the sequence right.

An A+ in this drill means you can do two continuous sets: three marching steps, three outside edge turns, three more marching steps, and three outside edge turns. Did you pass?

Practice this drill over a couple of days and don't frustrate yourself. This drill will click, just trust the process and your ability. There is great elegance in this drill. It's a skill used more for recoveries than anything else and, in all-terrain skiing, recoveries are half the fun.

Stick with it. I've had skiers come up to me several years after I taught them this drill and they have finally figured it out. Now they ski with pride and grace.

ONE-LEGGED SKIING

In all the clinics I've coached and all the drills I've seen others devise, Rob Deslauriers holds the record for the most bizarre drill ever. We were coaching an Advanced Ski Clinic at Crested Butte Resort and we had a bunch of skiers in the top group who could rip it up! So it was a challenge to teach them – they could almost do it all.

> **Goal: To fine-tune the touch of rolling a flat ski to an edged ski**
>
> **Body Position: Ski only on one ski and make slalom turns**

Well, Rob took the group up the poma lift and down onto the headwall. Then he made everyone take off one ski, throw it down the hill, and ski down to it on one ski. I'm talking steep headwall skiing with one ski! This group survived to tell about it.

This drill will prepare you for skiing anything. Don't do it on a headwall; try it first on a gentle intermediate slope. Skiing on one ski is easy – trust me. The key is keeping your ski in the fall line; don't let it slide or skid across the hill.

If you were able to do the previous drill, this one is a piece of cake. Start to glide down on one ski, make a short radius slalom turn on the downhill ski, finish the turn by unweighting, and then roll your hip into the hill to turn on the outside edge of the same ski. No big deal.

Again, remember to make short radius turns and don't try to turn your ski as if you are traversing. Ski down

95

the hill in the fall line and make constant fluid turns. Keep the pace up, link the turns together, and use momentum to keep the turns flowing.

When you visualize this drill, do it from start to finish. Don't think — first one turn, then another turn – these turns are all related. Each one feeds off the next, as shown on the video. Mihaela can do this with both eyes closed.

One-legged skiing fine-tunes your balance, upper body positioning, power, fluidity, and agility. Making consistent fluid one-legged turns puts you in a league few skiers ever reach. This drill will help you adjust your line in moguls, trees, and during recoveries.

The skill that is learned from these last two drills is skiing on the uphill ski — a necessary skill if you want to consider the mountain your playground. Practice ONE-LEGGED SKIING on different terrain and watch your ability soar.

MOGUL WALK

If I can't ski powder, I'll ski moguls – I love 'em. The magic of dancing over and around obstacles with ease is a true joy. My friend Scott Brooksbank is an amazing mogul skier. Scott is as fluid and graceful as he was when we competed on the Pro Mogul Tour back in the 70s. To me, he illustrates agility.

Why? Because all great mogul skiers ski the moguls rather than letting the moguls ski them. And Scott does just that. He skis the moguls by carving his turns down the back side of the bumps. His feet never leave the snow.

Goal: To demonstrate independent leg action in moguls

Body Position: In a mogul field, take 3 moving marching steps straight down the hill and then make 3 turns

A couple of years ago, I was skiing with Scott at an eastern resort where the bumps were less than perfect and Scott was flawless. At lunch, a young skier approached Scott and said, "I can never find the line you ski. How do you do it?" Scott replied, "Don't look for lines, mogul lines end where you want to start. Learn how to adapt to changing terrain through absorption and extensions, quick feet, and constant turns."

The MOGUL WALK is designed to develop quick feet and constant turns. It is the THREE-STEP TURN with moguls added. Find an intermediate mogul run, not too steep, with small bumps. Start by taking three marching steps and then make three slalom turns. Remember that you must adapt to the terrain, so you control the pace of the steps and the pace of the turns. I recommend that you think "Quick feet and fast turns."

The beauty of this drill is that you will seek out the path of least resistance, which will change between steps and turns. This proves that there is no one line through the moguls. Rather, using your mobility, fluidity, and agility, there are many. The illustrations on the cards and in the video show the consistency of the upper body and quick-moving feet in both the steps and turns.

Try and complete two sets in a row at a constant speed. Remember that you can control your speed with knee angulation, forcing pressure on your boot, which results in edge pressure against the snow.

Independent leg action in moguls is very important. It allows skiers to move laterally. It also increases stability since the skier is not deflecting his or her body from bump to bump. Instead the skier is absorbing, extending, and turning around and over the moguls.

This drill will develop reaction time and skiers can begin to increase their speed as long as the pace stays constant.

MIND OVER MOGUL

When I was a kid, my older brother once told me: "Ski the bumps as fast as you can until you fall, then pick yourself up and do it again. Pretty soon, you'll be skiing top to bottom and fast will seem normal and recoveries will be no big deal." So I took his advice, and it worked. But I was a kid then and able to bounce and bend in a lot of directions that I don't like to think about now.

MIND OVER MOGUL is a drill which has roots with this philosophy, but is just a little tamer. The goal of this drill is to ski within a confined space. This will force you to deal with everything in your path.

To start out, your confined area will be the entire width of the slope and, as you feel more comfortable, make the corridor narrower. Begin skiing in a mogul field and traverse from side to side on the trail making giant slalom turns. Practice absorbing the moguls as you traverse. When you are ready, make a turn and head in the other direction.

Goal: Finding your own path through the moguls

Body Position: Make large radius turns through the moguls

Make six to eight turns. Stop, regroup, and go again. Ski as wide as you like until you have no problems choosing where to turn. As you gain confidence, shorten your traverse but commit yourself to a certain space and a definite width. As you progress, bring your

99

commitment level higher by shortening the traverse until you are skiing the fall line.

This drill will build agility and identify the path of least resistance. You will instantly notice that moguls intimidate you less because you are learning where to turn.

The cool thing about this drill is that there are no standards or boundaries. Each skier's special style and path shines through. On the video, you can see that Mihaela and I have followed the path of least resistance.

Remember to keep your eyes looking down the fall line and past obstacles that intimidate you. MIND OVER MOGUL is great practice for all-terrain skiing.

MOGUL RIDE

For the last two drills, we have been skiing smooth and agile. Now we are going to add power and dynamic motion to our mogul skiing.

Start again by skiing the entire width of the slope and when it comes time to turn, ski up the back side of a mogul. As you reach the top, jump up and over the trough. Land on the back side of the following mogul.

This is a POWER TURN drill in the mogul. When you see a good mogul to launch off, jump up and down the fall line to initiate the turn. Land in the Power Position; absorb the impact of the landing and turn simultaneously. Let the speed of your traverse carry you over the trough.

> **Goal: To build power and agility into your mogul skiing**
>
> **Body Position: Make large radius turns through the moguls and initiate the turns by jumping up and down the fall line**

Practice this drill. The hardest part is timing your jump so that you land on the back side of the next bump. As your confidence grows, begin to shorten your traverse and ski more fall line. This skill is used in mogul skiing when you need to jump over a trough or bumps which otherwise would have caused disruption to your run. Most skiers are thrown off balance by obstacles they could have jumped over. The distance of the jump is determined more by the length of your skis than the height achieved in the jump. Let momentum and gravity carry you past ugly troughs and bumps. Your skis are long enough to bridge the gap; momentum is your friend. The combination will result in an undisrupted mogul run.

Take your time; be dynamic and loose. Review the POWER TURN drill if you are having any problems. MOGUL RIDE builds the agile, mobile, dynamic movements needed for all-terrain skiing.

Cut cards with scissors or knife along perforations. Do not rip cards from binding.
Card surfaces are weatherproof. For best protection place clear tape over card edges.

◇ 3

Dan Egan's Chairlift Guide to Skiing
AGILITY – 3 Step Outside Turn

GOAL:
To trust your reaction time.

BODY POSITION:
Three moving, marching steps, then three turns on the outside edge of the uphill ski.

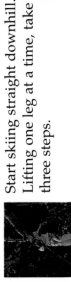

Start skiing straight downhill. Lifting one leg at a time, take three steps.

After the third step, make three turns using only the outside edges of the skis.

This requires hip angulation and keeping your skis in the fall line.

Roll your hip to the outside ski's edge and use your downhill ski for balance. Repeat until comfortable with the drill.

CARD 17A

1

Dan Egan's Chairlift Guide to Skiing
AGILITY – Thousand Steps

GOAL:
To establish agile, independent leg action.

BODY POSITION:
Make large radius turns, and keep legs walking throughout the whole run.

Start off traversing across the hill, making quick little steps.

Initiate your first turn while continuing to make quick little steps.

In the middle of the turn it is important to remain balanced while still making quick steps.

If at any point during the turn you were unable to continue stepping, you were out of balance.

CARD 16A

7

Dan Egan's Chairlift Guide to Skiing
FLUIDITY – Turns Within a Turn

GOAL:
To teach selective edge pressuring.

BODY POSITION:
Make medium radius turns, with rhythm changes during the traverse.

Make a turn using knee angulation. Then, traverse the hill.

Now initiate a turn but don't finish it.

Go back to a traverse.

Initiate a turn for the second time and complete it. Repeat the drill in the other direction.

CARD 15A

Cut cards with scissors or knife along perforations. Do not rip cards from binding. Card surfaces are weatherproof. For best protection place clear tape over card edges.

AGILITY - One Legged Skiing ◀ 4

GOAL:
To fine tune the touch of rolling a flat ski to an edged ski.

BODY POSITION:
Ski only on one ski and make slalom turns.

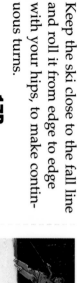

Start off in a balanced stance on one ski.

Make a turn using the inside edge, but don't let the ski cross the fall line too much.

Turn in the opposite direction on the outside edge by rolling your hip to the outside of the ski.

Keep the ski close to the fall line and roll it from edge to edge with your hips, to make continuous turns.

17B

AGILITY - 3 Step Turn 2

GOAL:
To enhance reaction time through change in rhythm.

BODY POSITION:
Make three moving, marching steps then make three turns.

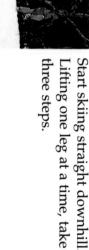

Start skiing straight downhill. Lifting one leg at a time, take three steps.

After your third step, make three turns using knee angulation.

After completing the third turn, straighten, then make three more steps.

After the third step, make three more turns. To control your speed, use more knee angulation and forward pressure.

16B

FLUIDITY - Javelin Turn ◆ 8

GOAL:
To reinforce hip angulation and stability at high speeds.

BODY POSITION:
Large radius turns, start turn on the uphill ski with the downhill ski off the snow.

While traversing across the hill, step up onto your uphill ski. Lift your downhill ski off the snow and place the tip across the uphill ski.

Roll your hip downhill and make a turn.

Uncross your skis, step up onto the new uphill ski, and repeat the drill.

Learn to trust hip angulation for stability.

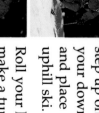

15B

Non-Stop Skiing

My Grandfather used to tell me this story over and over when I was a child. "There was a man walking down Beacon Street in Boston carrying a trumpet case." He would start, pause, and look at me like Granddads do, and say, "and a boy came up to him and asked, 'Excuse me, mister. Do you know how to get to Symphony Hall?' and the man replied, 'Practice, son, practice.'"

And that story says it all. Skiers of all ages have asked me, "How did you get so good? When did it all come together?" The truth of the matter is that skiing is about mileage, laps, and vertical feet. First one on the lift, last one off, as often as you can.

> **Goal: To experience changing terrain, conditions, and speed**
>
> **Body Position: Ski non-stop off of the lift for three runs in a row**

In high school, I took my friend Dave Zeering skiing. He was a great basketball player. After lunch, he said, "Dude, your boots are your sneakers. You are so comfortable in and on that equipment it's amazing. You can't jump in my basketball shoes and I can't ski in your boots."

Non-Stop Skiing is about making your boots feel like your sneakers. Ski top to bottom for two or three runs non-stop. Let your mind go and feel the sensation of skiing. Be a passenger along for the ride. Marvel at the performance of your skis and body working as one. Breathe in the speed and relax your mind.

NON-STOP SKIING is the best way to build confidence and a sense of your ability to ski within the Zone of Excellence. You have to experience the body's instinctive reactions and trust those reactions. Skiing is muscle memory. This drill is a combination of the whole package. The way to teach muscle memory is to repeat the motions, skills, and drills in this book. As your muscle memory expands, so will your ability. When you ski within your Zone of Excellence, it is as large as you make it, so, practice, practice, practice.

Skiing is about freedom, the forces of a turn, the power of the ski edging, the dynamic motion of your body responding to the slope, and your mind awakening to speed.

The mountains are your playground. Express yourself. Bring your style to them and enjoy NON-STOP SKIING. The ultimate ski run has no translation from experience to words. So live it, love it, and ski it!

All-Terrain Ski Stories

Ski the Trees

Looking for a magical experience on skis? Ski the trees! When done safely and correctly, you'll savor the experience forever. Here are some helpful hints that will build your confidence and your tree-skiing skills.

Always ski trees within the ski area boundaries and check with the ski patrol for the best conditions. Two snow conditions must exist before you can enter the woods. One, a deep base of snow is important to cover up stumps, rocks, and fallen trees; two, untracked snow to help keep your speed down.

Ski your favorite trail and pick a line close to the trees, regardless of the fall line, for at least 15 to 20 turns. Practice stopping within the line you have committed to skiing. Stopping is one of the most important skills you need to master. Don't progress to the glades until you are able to stop on a dime in any situation. Once you feel comfortable stopping in the line you have committed to, you are ready to start skiing through the glades.

Find some glades within the boundaries of a ski area, and begin your run six or seven turns above some tight trees. Visualize your path. Identify a safe place to stop. Ski the fall line. Make slalom turns at a consistent speed through the trees. Keep your head up. Look down the hill and concentrate only on the open spaces – don't stare at the trees. Stop five to six turns below the tight space you just skied through.

Do this over and over again until you are able to ski the glades, fall line, across the fall line, and a combination of both. Your success will depend on your ability to stop within the line you commit to skiing. Seasoned tree skiers stop in the middle of their line if they need to regroup; you can't afford to be even slightly out of control in the trees.

As you feel more comfortable in confined spaces, search the glades for tighter trees and longer alleyways. Ski at a slower pace than normal to increase your reaction time to the changing terrain. Your ability to make split-second decisions about which path to take around trees and over fallen logs will determine your progress. In the trees, you only have four options: left, right, straight, and stop. Side-stepping is also an effective tool to use when the trees become too tight.

There are 12 rules to skiing the trees beyond the boundaries. Please follow them all for your safety.

1. Check with the ski patrol to find out which woods are legal to ski.

2. Check with the ski patrol to make sure conditions are right and safe.

3. Never ski the woods alone.

4. Never enter the woods after 2:45 p.m., even with a partner.

5. Always wear goggles.

6. Ski with your pole straps off your wrists.

7. Enter only through open ski patrol gates and obey all posted signs.

8. Know where you are going and where you can exit the woods.

9. Have visual contact with your partner at all times.

10. Know how to do kick turns in both directions.
11. Tree skiing is for advanced skiers only.

12. Ski only as fast as the slowest person in the group.

To become an accomplished tree skier takes years of practice. You will encounter numerous conditions that will require several types of turning techniques. You must be well balanced and able to adapt the width of your turns while not increasing your speed. You must develop a keen sense of what is skiable and what is not. Most importantly, you must realize that sometimes side-stepping and traversing are the best options for safety reasons. Don't try to ski anything you're not comfortable with. Peer pressure can cause injury: think for yourself and ski smart.

Extreme Dreaming in Turkey

Out of the corner of my eye I saw a gun, and it was pointed right at my brother John's head. He was riding in the front passenger seat.

"Get out and push!" Very deliberate and very clear came the words from the man with the gun, our gruff Turkish taxi driver. We all snapped to attention. The van was a wave of movement but John just sat there, staring straight ahead.

It was 8:15 a.m. We had been on a smoke-filled bus for over ten hours traveling from Bursa, near the coast, to Kayseri in Central Anatolia. We had made the mistake of renting the first mini van we found to take us to Mt. Erciyes, (3,916 meters), an extinct volcano with a chairlift and a T-bar, two hours away.

The real problem with the mini van was not that it was the first one we came across, but that it had bald tires and a driver who had no clue about how to drive on icy roads. And, of course, an hour into the trip we were on a windy, icy mountain road and every time we hit a patch of ice, the driver would punch the gas pedal and spin the tires. Eventually it happened: our Turkish chauffeur parked us into the biggest snow bank he could find and we were stuck.

The wind howled outside and shook the van; it was miserable outside, cold and windy with drifting snow. No one spoke. No one moved.

The whole film crew seemed to groan at once but, before we got out, we struck a deal. "Leave the gun on the dash where we can see it and we'll push." The gun, a nine-millimeter, was left on the console, but our driver took the bullet clip and put it in his pocket.

Waist deep in snow, avalanche shovels in hand, we dug and pushed. Several times we freed the van and several times the Turk planted it in a different part of the snow bank. Finally, after untangling the chains and banning the driver from the wheel, we were able to escape with the help of a passing oil truck that pulled us up the steepest part of the road.

Mt. Erciyes has two hotels, one for the public and one for the government officials and workers who keep the road clear. We were eager to check in, but once the public hotel realized we were Americans, they raised the price up five times the regular cost. So I set out for the government hotel armed with one of our guides, Hakan.

We soon became guests of the official government hotel. The film crew plus our two guides, seven altogether, had two rooms for a reasonable price of $6.00 a day per person including meals.

We were all dead tired and as the crew headed out to get some lunch, John pulled me aside, leaned up against the wall, and said, "Just another typical film shoot for Warren Miller."

"Ya," I said, "cornices and avalanches seem mellow compared to crazed taxi drivers with guns."

"Ah, life wouldn't be worth living if you didn't get to face death once in a while," he replied.

The lunch room was big and buzzing with weekend excitement. It was Friday and families were enjoying a traditional noontime meal of vegetables, soup, salad, and bread.

The bright sun warmed the room as we all ate in awed silence, gazing out the window at the huge volcanic cone covered with snow. It was dominating. We had come a long way for age-old reasons: to experience a new mountain culture and to connect with ourselves in the mountains. To find that feeling of comfort mountain people know and understand.

The next day, we were all rested and the ski area was alive with a refreshing pulse. Tom Grissom, our cameraman, was running around filming the morning flow of skiers as they flocked around the outdoor rental shop. He yelled, "Warren will love this. Oh yeah, Warren will flip out!"

It was a scene like no other we had ever seen in our travels. The parking attendants were military men with machine guns, smiling and helping people with their equipment. The outdoor rental shop had skis laid out on the snow with the boots in the bindings. People were standing around in their stockings, stepping in and out of boots until they found a pair that fit. Then off they would go with two different-sized poles and huge smiles on their faces.

Parents pulled kids on sleds, teenagers laughed and pushed their way through the long lift line. The single chairlift crept along at a standstill pace running on a backup two-stroke engine. Turkish music crackled through the sound system which had speakers on every chairlift tower. It took almost thirty-three minutes to the top, over twice as long as the T-bar which went to the same place. I rode the lift twice; I felt as if I were on a different planet. It was simply amazing – what a scene.

Here we were in central Anatolia where the skiers had no preconceptions about the sport. They were free of the fashion requirements, glamour, and glitz we deal with here in the United States. They were skiing on antique equipment: boots with no buckles, clothing ranging from wool pants to vintage ski fashions from

111

the 1960s. One guy even used two tree branches for poles.

Wade McKoy, still photographer on assignment for *Skiing* magazine, was snapping pictures like crazy. Josh Lerman, also from *Skiing* magazine, was interviewing Turkish ski instructors. Dean Decas, our video man, was mobbed with requests to tape smiling, friendly Turks who wanted to be American film stars.

John and I were busy making friends with a small group of young skiers ranging in age from ten to twelve. They were showing us around the mountain, leading us to all of their favorite jumps and bumps. We communicated with sign language, smiles, and laughter. We were part of their little gang for about an hour and three quarters. We were enchanted with their ability to feel life and explore new things. They would experiment with what little English they knew and were so proud when we understood them. Waving goodbye to them as they ran off to lunch, John said, "Kids are kids." We laughed.

We spent the afternoon high above the chairlift checking out descents off the back of the mountain. After digging several snow pits and studying the snow pack, we felt comfortable about filming there the next day.

John and I sat on top for a while studying the different couloirs there were to ski — some with cliffs in the middle and some with cornices on top. We felt free, at peace, lost in our own thoughts. We knew this would be our best chance to ski without the cameras around. We lived for opportunities like this.

John didn't have to say a thing when he stood up and grabbed his equipment. I knew what he was thinking and I knew he had found his line. I watched. He climbed further up to the top of the couloir, strapped on his backpack, checked his avalanche beeper, gave me the standard double click of the ski poles, and jumped off the cornice. I could feel his turns, checking his speed as he dropped off a little eight-foot rock in the middle of the chute and continued skiing. His laughter was echoing off the valley walls and I laughed too. I picked up my equipment in a trance and headed off to my line, the one I had visualized in my head for the last half hour.

Giving my equipment a final check, I heard John yell, "It looks sweet, brother." I gave him the over-the- head double pole click and jumped in. It was steep; the snow started to sluff with me on every turn; I felt relaxed and knew that I had found what I had come for. I became lost in my own echoes off the valley wall, my legs pumped with adrenaline like so many times before. No thoughts or words can explain it. I skied up to John who was bursting with excitement and joy. We both screamed and laughed and knew we had a long hike out but didn't care. We were somewhere in central Anatolia, Turkey, and we were living our own extreme dream.

Mysteries of the
Transylvanian Alps, Romania

Four of us had just climbed to the top of tram tower number three, at the Sinaia Ski Resort in the Transylvania Alps in Romania. I was standing in silence next to Rob DesLauriers, staring out at the horizon, searching for a skiable patch of snow. In my mind I kept hearing a voice that said, "Wanderlust, 30 feet of snow in Squaw Valley, California, record winter in Sugarbush, Vermont, and Warren Miller sends us to Romania with not a flake of snow in sight."

Cameraman Mike Graber was on the far side of the platform, climbing over the railing which hung 175 feet above a snowless ski trail. Our still photographer was snapping photos of the resort down below. The mood was somber, no one spoke, but I knew we were all thinking the same thing, "How can we make a ski movie without snow!"

Back down in the hotel, I heard Mike say to my brother John, "We have twelve days to search these mountains and find snow, start looking under the rocks."

Down the hall, Eric DesLauriers yelled. "I can't believe there's no snow! I want Tahoe!" The trip was only three days old — his words hung in the air and seemed to challenge each one of us.

The quest had begun and slowly each member of our crew turned the initial shock of the lack of snow into a crusade to band together and make the film work. Our over-stuffed rental van rolled along over the twisting mountain road, with voices crying out, "Over there, look! A couloir with snow!" or "Hey, the north side of that face has snow, let's hike."

114

We crept into a small mountain town called Predal, the town with the highest elevation in the Transylvanian Alps and a ski resort. The Predal ski area had one chairlift and a T-Bar. Base elevation was 1,650 meters; the agonizing 27-minute lift ride took you to the top at 2,048 meters. At the bottom of the chairlift, military men gathered with prehistoric ski equipment. At the top, the lift-op was a shepherd who kept a wagon full of hay next to the lift shack with his horses and dogs running about. We felt out of place, but from our new vantage point we could see snow-covered peaks and our spirits were fueled.

Skiing in Predal was sketchy: cover was thin and rocks were plentiful. In the trees, the snow was deeper and untouched. John however, had found some bushes under the lift and bounced his way down through them, turning lightly, making it look easy. I attempted a variation of the same line. Gaining speed, I pressured my skis too hard on the next turn and double heels released. Slamming my face into four inches of old snow, I tumbled to a stop. Standing up slowly, dazed and confused, I realized I had not adjusted the tension of my bindings on my newly mounted skis. It was day four; I felt an already long trip getting longer.

Rob DesLauriers and our video man, Dean Decas, had a good laugh for themselves at my expense. I retrieved my good humor, my skis and poles, and dusted myself off and skied away. As I skied up to John he said, "Carving with your nose again?" We laughed and went to adjust my bindings.

It started snowing on day five. We couldn't believe it, but down it came and pile up it did! We had found our third ski area, Pioana Brasov, rumored to be the Aspen of Romania and home to the national ski team.

This ski area had an identity crisis: there was an old two-seater gondola that looked like it was out of a 1932 movie and two trams, one of which was bright pink. The national ski team was equally strange to us because they used branches for gates. Watching ski racers carrying bundles of sticks onto a pink tram, Eric turned to Dean and said, "Now, there's a sight you don't see every day." Amongst that group was a young skier named Mihaela Fera.

Up on the mountain, the storm made it impossible to see. The skiing was acceptable, but once again we couldn't escape the rocks on the trail. After taking two runs, we decided we could film in the trees when the storm let up, so we set out to find a good meal and lodging for the night.

Following a tip from some fellow American travelers, we went directly to a small chalet and moved in. The owner was a small, tough mountain man who had built the chalet himself. His name was Cornelius, an Olympic ski jumper from the 1964 games in Innsbruck.

Speaking to us in German, he told us this story. On the day he started building the chalet, his wife went to town to gather some supplies. He said he was worried, because over the last 25 years he had made many changes to the chalet, adding on more rooms and, since his wife hadn't returned yet, she probably wouldn't bring back enough supplies!

The storm left six and a half inches behind and, next day, the skies were blue. Loading onto the second tram up the mountain in the morning, we were amazed at how few locals were up early to ski the fresh new snow. Our crew was chomping at the bit for fresh tracks but the few skiers around us seemed not to care.

We went directly into the trees where the snow was the deepest. There was a sense of urgency to make every shot work. We were skiing in pairs and working a rotation of skiing a line and hiking back up for another. We were kicking into a groove and it felt great!

Rob was on a mission to jump a cliff and, later in the day, his search paid off. Near the side of a trail, he discovered a small rock band, 13 feet high. It was not ideal: the take-off was blind, the flight was through some branches, and the landing was a bit flat. But the sky was blue, we needed a jump, and Rob was up for the flight.

He popped it perfectly, flying through the branches and landing on the last patch of untracked snow next to the trails and skied away. The Romanian skiers were watching in disbelief. Finally, a ski instructor stepped forward with some friendly words and then said, "I've skied this mountain for 15 years and never have I thought to jump off that pile of rocks." We all laughed and then our new friend offered to show us some secret powder stashes and we were off, back to the trees.

We were soon introduced to many local skiers and every day a crowd would gather to watch us film. When we were done with a jump, or had tracked up all the powder, a few of our new friends would attempt the same jump or ski the same line. It was constant entertainment and their energy levels fed into ours. It was fun and made us feel more at home.

The pieces were falling into place and it was feeling like a true blue Warren Miller film. The weather pattern was perfect: 24 hours of snow, two days of sun, followed by more snow. On the snowy days, we skied with the locals exploring the mountain and answering their many questions about skiing in the States. At night we would stumble our way through the Romanian menu, eat a meal, and then some of the film crew would gather in the disco with our new friends to experience the local night scene.

By Friday, day eleven, we found ourselves on top of the mountain at sunset with one day left on the trip. There was an orange glow on the snow. The cameras were across the valley set up for a big long shot of us skiing the face from the peak.

John and Eric went first. Once out of our sight, we could hear their voices echoing down the valley. Rob was leaning on his ski poles looking out at the sun. Lost in a late afternoon haze, I murmured to myself, "Wanderlust, Romania, Transylvanian Alps, mountain cultures..." and Rob muttered, "making movies..."

If You Go There...

In *The Real Guide to Eastern Europe*, we read that "Romania was once known as the 'Bread Basket of Europe,' now it is known as the 'Basket Case of Europe.'" We found that to be true as well. Traveling in Romania takes patience and a loose schedule. Double-check all your travel arrangements right up until the time you leave. Don't expect any fancy cultural experience or exotic foods. Your best bet is to go with a tour group.

There are two ski areas worth visiting. Sinaia Resort has a vertical drop of over 3,500 feet, four trams, two chairs, and six surface lifts. Sinaia was the winter home to the Romanian monarchs; the castle is a must-see and tours run daily.

Poiana Brasov is located a half hour from the city of Brasov. The resort has a pool, several hotels, small

**Cut cards with scissors or knife along perforations. Do not rip cards from binding.
Card surfaces are weatherproof. For best protection place clear tape over card edges.**

Egan Entertainment Network
800-619-6801

INSTRUCTIONAL PRODUCTS

A. Chairlift Ski Guide - From novice to expert, Dan Egan, Extreme Skier and his wife Mihaela, a three-time Romanian Olympic Skier, teach you the fundamentals of proper ski techniques. This coordinated guide includes a book (ALL TERRAIN SKIING), Training Video (complete with exercises) and 19 cards you can select drills from for your ride up the mountain.

Complete Set - $49.95
Book/Instruction Cards - $24.95
Video - $29.95

B. Advance To The Steeps - $29.95
Featuring Dan and John Egan, Rob and Eric DesLauriers and Dean Decas. Learn the secrets from the best all-terrain skiers in the world.

ACTION VIDEOS

C. The Extreme Dream: Price - $14.95
D. Return of the Shred-I: Price - $19.95
E Where The Steeps Have No Name - $19.95

KIDS VIDEOS

F. Children of the Snow: Price - $14.95

Order now by calling **1-(800) 619-6801**

Shipping and Handling Charges -

Merchandise Total	Add Shipping and Handling
$10.00 to $25.00	$3.50 per order
$26.00 and up	$5.00 per order

Allow 3 to 4 weeks for delivery.
American Express, Mastercard and Visa accepted.

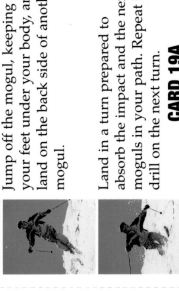

Dan Egan's Chairlift Guide to Skiing
AGILITY - Mogul Ride
7

GOAL:
To build power and agility into your mogul skiing.

BODY POSITION:
Large radius turns through the moguls. Initiate the turns by jumping off of a mogul.

Traverse the mogul field using constant fluid motion to absorb the moguls.

Keep your head up and eyes downhill while looking for a good mogul to jump off of.

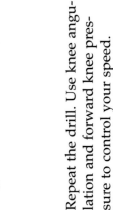

Jump off the mogul, keeping your feet under your body, and land on the back side of another mogul.

Land in a turn prepared to absorb the impact and the next moguls in your path. Repeat the drill on the next turn.

CARD 19A

Dan Egan's Chairlift Guide to Skiing
AGILITY - Mogul Walk
5

GOAL:
To demonstrate independent leg action in moguls.

BODY POSITION:
Take three moving, marching steps straight down the hill and then make three turns.

Take three steps through the moguls.

Make three turns through the moguls.

Repeat the drill. Use knee angulation and forward knee pressure to control your speed.

You determine where you want to turn, not the moguls. Ski the mountain, don't let the mountain ski you.

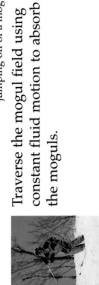

CARD 18A

Cut cards with scissors or knife along perforations. Do not rip cards from binding.
Card surfaces are weatherproof. For best protection place clear tape over card edges.

A

C

F

E

D

Dan Egan's Chairlift Guide to Skiing

AGILITY – Non-stop Skiing

◆ 8

GOAL:
To experience changing terrain, condition and speed.

BODY POSITION:
Ski non-stop off of the lift for three runs in a row.

Skiing non-stop forces you to react to the changes in terrain.

Skiing non-stop forces you to react to changes in conditions.

Skiing non-stop forces you to react to changes in speed.

Skiing non-stop forces you to react to the ever-changing situations on your journey down the mountain.

19B

Dan Egan's Chairlift Guide to Skiing

AGILITY – Mind Over Mogul

◆ 6

GOAL:
To find your own path through the moguls.

BODY POSITION:
Make large radius turns through the moguls.

Traverse the mogul field, absorbing the bumps.

Make a turn wherever it feels comfortable.

Traverse again, continuing to use constant fluid motion to absorb the bumps.

Make another turn using constant fluid motion to find your path of least resistance.

18B

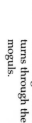

chalets, and a comfortable setting in the mountains. The resort is marketed very aggressively in England, so language is not a problem. The skiing is often excellent with many hidden spots. The majority of runs are intermediate. There are two trams, one chair, and four surface lifts.

It is worth spending a day or two in Bucharest, the capital. The aftermath of the five-day revolution of 1989 makes it a very interesting and historical trip. The train system is a good and inexpensive way to travel. Don't rent a car – it's too expensive and driving is too dangerous.

Our tour was arranged by S.K.I. Tours: call 1.800.842.7855. We didn't have great snow but it had been a real bad year in Europe. Normally, February and March are best for snowfall. If you go to Poiana Brasov, stay at the chalet across from the Alpine Hotel and tell Cornelius the Brothers say "Hi!"

In Your Wildest Dreams

It was 3:00 a.m. on Route 93 in the middle of Montana. We were heading north to go cat skiing at Island Lake in Fernie, British Columbia. While I jammed to music on the radio, the van suddenly started to slide out of control. The highway was covered with black ice. I tried not to panic. Then there was a startled silence as the van went into its first 360-degree spin. We were way overloaded with eight people, ski gear, and camera equipment, and I couldn't steer us straight. As the van crashed into the median, I could see nothing but white.

"We didn't tip over," yelled someone from the back. Then came a burst of nervous laughter and I slowly released my death grip on the steering wheel. It was bone-chilling cold outside; the wind howled; and the van was stuck firmly in a bank of fresh snow.

Barely awake, my brother John got out and said with an odd look in his eye, "We'll have fresh tracks tomorrow if we can get out of here tonight."

It took all eight of us digging and pushing for a half hour to finally free the van. Ah, the power of powder. But six and a half hours later, at 9:30 a.m., you could feel the energy flowing in everyone. The diesel engine of the cat surged ahead and we were on our way up the mountain. "It's hard to explain to anyone who doesn't ski," I thought, "but when there is prime powder snow to be had, no obstacle is too great. We just about carried that van back onto the highway."

Snapping into our skis at the top of the mountain, cameraman Tom Grissom said, "Warm-up run, we'll film later." There on location in Island Lakes to shoot a segment of our new film "The Extreme Dream," we were all about to experience some extreme powder. On our first cruise through the trees, everyone was excited. We had brought long-time gravity slaves Wolfgang and Ken Robinson out to do their first film shoot ever.

Both Sugarbush, Vermont, locals, these two snowboarders were at home in the trees: carving, jumping, and railsliding all the way down the mountain. Tom later turned to me and said, "Great choice, these guys rip."

It was a perfect day for filming, face shots at every turn. Ken and Wolfgang were doing it all. Filming isn't easy. You have to know where the camera is at all times, where the shot can happen, and when to turn it on. These two shred heads were naturals. Their style and personality really shone through as they cruised the untracked terrain.

Kenny is a cook at a Mexican restaurant in the Mad River Valley. Motivated like so many other resort locals all around the world, he works to snowboard and snowboards to live. It's a beautiful thing, a simple life with a free lift pass, meals at work, and endless days of boarding. Ken has a constant smile on his face and if he isn't talking about snowboarding, he's thinking about it.

Fellow boardmaster and powder hound Wolfgang is a legend in the Mad River Valley. This guy can ski, telemark, and snowboard as well as anyone alive. He lives for fresh snow. Whether it's knee deep or the fluff on the side of the trail, Wolfgang knows where to find the fresh stuff. He has held every job imaginable to support his many hobbies. Wolfgang windsurfs and skateboards all summer, then plays in the snow for the rest of the year. At 37, he's the biggest kid I've ever met.

To John and myself, these two guys represent the reasons why so many people love ski movies. They are passionate about their sport and will do anything to keep their dreams alive. I could see by the smiles on their faces that Island Lake's waist-deep powder was all they needed to make their day.

One morning, I was awakened by a loud "Ya-hoooo" outside my window. Rubbing the sleep from my eyes, I couldn't believe what I was witnessing. Dawn was just breaking and Wolfgang and Kenny had built a jump and were blasting down the hill off the jump and landing in the new powder that had fallen overnight.

John came bursting into my room, laughing. "You see those nuts? We're up here for a week of incredible powder skiing, with a private snow cat, and these guys are up at dawn swimming in it." We both yelled out the window to the powder pigs below. Wolfgang turned to us and answered, "Hey, in your wildest dreams, you got to live it and love it."

Skier's Syndrome: Skiers' Denial

It's August: hazy, hot, and humid. My body is on the beach but my mind is bouncing between mashing moguls, climbing mountains, and the refreshing feeling of powder chilling my cheeks. These are the days that test skiers' souls. Ever since the last skiable patch of snow melted on the headwall in Tuckerman's Ravine, I've been suffering from what I call "Skier's Denial."

Every year it starts around mid-June. I mountain bike with the single track junkies through black fly season, covering myself with mud and sweat. Then I climb on my road bike, pounding out mile after mile with road warriors four to five times a week, trying to outrace the mosquitoes into July. After the Fourth, I call anyone with a power boat and tow rope and waterski into the cool summer twilight.

When August hits, I settle for long naps in between short walks on the beach. I can no longer hide the fact that I long to ski and no other activity can take its place. Very few of my friends can relate because my outward actions and my endless search for physical pleasures seem to say, "I'm having fun, I love the summer." But the reality is that I'm heavily into denial – Skiers' Denial — a state of mind not understood by the conventional thinkers or the medical field.

I first became aware of this syndrome five years ago. I had traveled quite a distance one weekend to hang out with some of my hardcore ski buddies. We had all the toys: windsurfers, trampoline, volleyball, frisbees, and loud music. It was a festival of sorts with strumming guitars, jugglers, and, of course, a good old New England lobster bake.

Friday night was filled with the excitement of seeing old friends, setting up camp, and telling a few lies. Saturday morning, the place erupted with activity. For starters, a good morning swim followed by waterskiing on the smooth lake surface. The mid-morning mountain bike ride proved to be a test of the male egos, everyone trying to outsprint the next guy up and down the hilly terrain of New Hampshire. Stopping just long enough to refuel for lunch because the wind had picked up, we all raced to rig our sailboards and skip across the rippling water.

By six o'clock, we all sat on the beach staring out across the lake. It was story time – tall tales of the day's adventures, with the conversation going off on different tangents and the endless laughter carrying across to the distant shore. After a while, the chatter tailed off and the wind began to die down. Billy piped up from the middle of the group and said, "Ya, it was a full day, but nothing like the time we all skied bottomless powder up in Grand Targhee, Wyoming, last February."

The group all responded with a silent nod. I can't speak for the others but I smiled a deep, bright smile within my soul. In no time, I was recalling the endless powder runs, floating turn after turn and feeling free, letting gravity pull my body through the white gold on the ground.

The memory stalled the hands of time and I laid in a blissful state of powder turns gone by. Then suddenly, a voice violated my world: "Hey. Look at all of you guys," should Pat. "lost in a haze of thought triggered by a memory at least six months old. It's summer time, man, it's warm, sunny, and we're all on a beach. What are you guys – in some sort of denial?"

"Ya, Skiers' Denial," muttered Billy, "Skiers' Denial."

"That must be what it is," mumbled Denis. "And no matter what, nothing will ever replace the unexplainable feeling of gliding down a mountain leaving your own personal signature carved into the pristine white snow. I for one love it, call it what you want – Skiers' Denial or a desire for internal peace. I long for the season all winter and I've been praying for snow since April."

It was right then and there that I realized I'm a skier and I've been going left and right ever since the age of five. The only language I know is spoken in the mountains, amongst the snow, trees, wind, while I'm on my skis. I've stood on top of mountains all over the world. Smiled at others who understand the feeling of a smooth turn in soft snow, laughed when the snow went down my neck, and cried every spring when the birds began to chirp and sing. The rivers run wild when the weather turns mild, washing away my stage built out of the substance we call snow.

I don't care for harsh words or petty games. It's skiing where my heart remains. Free to go fast or slow, it's skiing that makes me feel just so. But every summer around about June, my mind remembers a happier tune of times gone past. Then the dreams begin of a season when the air turns cold and the hearty stand boldly on mountains everywhere waiting, willing, to venture out and free their souls.

Skiing is simple, and I like that and if it means suffering through the Dog Days of Summer, then so be it. Winter will come, the snow will fall, and all will be right when the summit is in sight.

Training

Blueprint for Conditioning

1. Routine

Define the time, place, and activity that fits your schedule. The important thing is not the length of the workout but the consistency of the activity.

2. Repetition

Skiing is based on simple body movements done over and over. It's important to condition your mind and body to perform an activity many times over. No matter what the activity is – golf, tennis, in-line skating – think about the repetition of body mechanics.

3. Fun

The ultimate goal is to enjoy ourselves. Too many people get caught up in performance and lose sight of the experience.

4. Patience

Conditioning and getting your body in shape take time. Don't get frustrated and don't overdo it. Pace yourself and be committed to the long-term goal of overall fitness.

5. Workout Partners

Work out with a friend. It will make time pass quicker and you'll enjoy the process more. Working out with a friend will help you stay motivated and committed.

Dryland Training

As a child, every corner in the house became a ski gate. Patterns in the rug became moguls to turn around; stairs became steep pitches to bounce down. Every little game increased my body awareness to the point that I had to think less about my technical skiing and more about having fun. I still apply that childish play to my workouts today. Here are some fun ways to keep workouts interesting and, at the same time, to work on being balanced.

The best part about these drill is that you don't need a gym or special equipment, just your creative mind and the great outdoors. I find that once I get started on some of these games, new ones pop up and the drills become more difficult and better for my skiing.

Next time you go out jogging, in-line skating, or just walking down the stairs, hold your hands out as if you have ski poles and imagine yourself skiing. Make this a habit – it will help you with your upper body position on snow. I find simulating my upper body position jogging, in-line skating uphill, or walking up stairs very challenging.

On Sunday mornings, in the city, work out in empty parking lots. The painted parking line can be used like a balance beam. Skip twice on your left foot and switch to skipping twice on your right foot along a painted line – this is great for balance. Jump up on your left leg, spin around 180 degrees, and land on your right leg on the painted line. Try to keep your hands in a skiing position and don't look down at the lines — look up.

Baseball fields are great for skiing workouts. You can jog the bases backwards. Hop on one leg to first, then on the other to second, and switch all the way around the bases. Concentrate on your upper body for balance. Use the dugout benches for a balance beam. Go the length hopping on one leg, then switch to the other leg, or try mixing it up just like the parking lot line drill.

Hiking in the mountains is an incredible way to work on your balance. Jump on and off logs, over logs, or practice mid-air tucks while jumping over the log. Dance around trees like slalom gates. Jump up and grab for branches as you run by, but try to keep stride and not be thrown off balance.

Beaches are a cool place to train. At low tide, the sand is great for barefoot running. Play the wave game. Facing the water, run toward the water when the wave goes out and run backwards when the wave comes in. If the wave catches you, you're out. Jog in the water about ankle deep (remember to hold your ski poles), slowly venture out to about mid-calf. This is great exercise – you'll get tired quickly. Don't worry about how far you can run; try it at different depths, but remember that the deeper you go, the harder it is, so take your time and remember to rest.

Stand on a dock at a lake or a diving board at a pool. Run and jump into the water, but while you are in the air, pull your knees up to your chest and extend them before you hit the water. Now do it again and see how many times you can clap your hands before you hit the water. Next time, grab your feet in mid-flight. Practice your favorite jump, double daffy, or try a 360. Play – it is a blast to see how many things you can do in the air before hitting the water.

The most important element in improving your balance is becoming comfortable with your own body's movement. Anything you can do to increase your body awareness is good for you on skis. Train with a friend; make it a game of seeing who can out-balance the other, use each other as a measure for your own improvements. Most of all, think skiing. Look at photographs of balanced skiers, watch movies, and have images in your mind when you train. Have fun and get in balance – even out of season.

Ski Training

By Drew Craig, Professional Trainer

Summer is a memory. Each night is a little cooler. You have had only one thing on your mind for the last month – skiing! Well, it is time to do more than just think skiing. Now is the time to get your muscles and mind tuned for skiing!

It doesn't take much to get started. You have most of what is necessary: muscles, desire, and a good pair of sneakers. If you have a bike or in-line skates, that's a bonus! (If you don't, it could be a good reason to try them.) Some other useful equipment includes dumbbells, exertubes®, or dynabands®.

Things to remember when involved in any training program:

- Check with your doctor, especially if you have had any injuries or illnesses.
- Always warm up first – do any light activity using large muscle groups for five to ten minutes.
- Stretch the muscles you will be using for that activity.
- Cool down after you work out with some light activity and stretching.
- Start slowly and concentrate on proper form.

Aerobic Conditioning: (running, biking, in-line skating) These are great exercises for heart and lung fitness as well as ski fitness. (In-line skating is the closest to skiing in form and function.) When using these activities for training, keep skiing in mind. What do I mean? There is no reason to run a marathon. Instead, try varying intensities, for example:

- long slow distance (maximum five miles)
- interval run – slow steady pace with short maximal effort sprints, then back to slow pace
- uphill run – run up, walk down

Aerobic training should be done at 65-75 percent of your maximum heart rate for 30 minutes to one hour. (For a rough estimate of your maximum heart rate, subtract your age from 220.)

Ski Exercises

Lateral Jumps: Feet shoulder-width apart, arms relaxed and bent at the elbows; bend at knees, push off the inside of your left foot toward your right as far as you can. Land on your right foot, push off the inside of your right foot immediately.

Box Jumps: Set up a rope or box at a height you can comfortably jump over (make sure it will come loose should you land on it; cinder blocks are not a good idea). Get in your skier stance, keeping your upper body still. Jump with both feet over the rope or box and immediately jump back.

Downhill Jumps: From a proper tuck position, jump straight up as high as possible. Absorb landing with entire body; immediately jump back up.

Ski Squats: Hold onto a bar or railing for support, feet shoulder-width apart. On one leg, slowly lower body. Keep your heel flat, your back straight, and your knee behind your toes. Lower until your thigh is parallel to the floor. Keep the other foot tucked behind your ankle.

Side Lunges: Feet shoulder-width apart, toes pointed slightly outward; step with one foot out to the side.

Bend that knee and bring weight onto that leg. Push back to start. Repeat on the other side. Keep your back straight, upper body facing forward, knees behind your toes, heel of back foot flat.

Strength Exercises

There are many good strength exercises depending on the equipment you have available. Listed below are exercises you can do at home with little or no equipment. Use of dumbbells or exercise tubing is beneficial but not necessary.

Push-Up or Chest Press: Keep your back flat, elbows out, push body or dumbbells straight up.

Chair Dips: Set up two chairs, one to put your feet on, the other behind you to rest your hands on. Slowly lower yourself until your elbows are almost shoulder level. Push up to start position.

Arm Curl: Arms hanging by your side, palms facing toward hips, keep elbows by sides, raise hands thumbs up, halfway through movement, turn palms toward body. Continue raising to shoulders. Lower slowly. Dumbbells or exercise tubing can be used.

Upright Row: Hands in front of body at shoulder width, leading with the elbows; pull up until hands are under chin. Elbows should be higher than your hands. Lower and repeat. Dumbbells or exercise tubing can be used.

Pull-Ups: Any door frame or bar that can support your weight. With palms facing away and hands apart wider than your shoulders, take a firm grip but do not over-squeeze. Pull up to your chin. Lower and repeat.

Single Arm Row: Use a dumbbell, exercise tubing, or even a jug filled with water. On a bench or chair, support your body on one knee and hand, let the other arm hang from the shoulder. Pull up keeping the elbow close to the body until your hand comes up to your lower ribs. Slowly lower. Switch sides.

Outer Hip: Put your ski boots on (doesn't that feel great!). Lying on your side, life your top leg as high as possible. Slowly lower and repeat. Switch sides.

Inner Hip: From the same position as above, lift the lower leg up and lower slowly. Move the upper leg forward and bend the knee.

Abs: Lying on your back, knees bent, feet flat, hands across chest, tighten stomach muscles and slowly raise head and shoulders. Pause and slowly lower. Repeat.

Obliques: Lying on your side with knees bent, shoulders flat on the floor, raise head and shoulders straight up. Lower slowly. Switch sides.

How many do you do?

Beginner: 1 set of each 8-10 repetitions

THE WORKOUT

Monday:	Interval run; ski exercises; abs
Tuesday:	Strength
Wednesday:	Long slow distance, abs
Thursday:	Strength; ski exercises
Friday:	Uphill run; abs
Saturday:	Go for a hike
Sunday:	Rest

Here is one final note: the best thing you can do for any sport is to cross-train. In other words, stay active all year. Try as many different activities as possible. Be adventurous, try something new. You just might surprise yourself. See you out there!

Mihaela's Guide to Training

1. Leg Flexibility and Stretching

From a standing position, take a big step forward so that the back foot is slightly on its toes. Your upper body should be straight with arms at your side. Slowly bring your body down until the front thigh is parallel to the floor. (If your knee is past your toes at this point, you need to take a bigger step.) At the same time, move your arms in an arcing motion above your head and slightly arch backwards. Return to the start position and turn so that the back foot is now in front and repeat motion. (10 times)

2. Breathing with Your Whole Body

In your normal walking stride, take three steps forward. On the third step, take a deep breath while moving your arms in an arcing motion above your head. Exhale as you bring your arms down and continue walking. Repeat. (10 times)

3. Leg Flexibility and Strength

In a pace slightly faster than your normal walking pace, take three steps forward. On the third step, bring your right leg up in a kicking motion. Keep your toes pointed out until you reach the top of the kick, then pull your toes toward your shin. As you are kicking, bring your left arm over to reach your toes. Keep both knees straight during the kick and do not bend at the waist. Continue walking and repeat with your opposite leg. (5 times for each leg)

4. Legs and Balance

Start with your right foot one step back. Step back far enough to stretch your leg. The left knee should be bent. Swing your right leg forward and up, keeping the toes pointed and knee straight. Straighten your left knee as you kick. As you reach the top of the kick, touch your toes with your left

136

hand. Return to the start position and repeat. Switch legs after all repetitions are done.

5. **Advanced Legs and Balance**
Same exercise as above without pausing or touching the ground at start position (continuous leg swing). Knees are kept straight.

6. **Advanced Balance**
Start with the right foot in front of the left and off the ground. Arms are raised out to the side. Raise your right leg laterally toward your hand as high as you can without bending at the waist. Keep both knees straight. Your ankle should be slightly higher than your toes. Return to start position and repeat. Switch legs after all repetitions are done. Keep body balanced and straight.

7. **Strength and Balance**
Start with feet spread laterally as wide as you are comfortable with. Your feet should be flat. Bring your body down and toward your right knee. If this causes your knee to go past your toes, you are bringing your body too far forward. Keep the left knee straight and foot flat. Touch left elbow to right knee. Return to start position; repeat on other leg.

8. **Advanced Strength and Balance**
Same starting position as above. Bring your body down toward right knee and grab the right ankle with your right hand (grab the ankle from the front). Then lean toward your left. Return to starting position and repeat on other leg.

Five Tips for Buying Equipment

1. Read pre-season magazine guides.

Starting in August, ski magazines publish extensive equipment review issues. The amount of information covered can be overwhelming. To eliminate confusion, identify your needs. Know your ability and read only what pertains to you.

2. Visit a couple of ski shops and make friends with at least one salesperson per shop.

Ski shop employees are a valuable resource and can help you weed through the technobabble in the magazines. Take time to wander into the shops first to make some acquaintances and then to ask questions. When you feel comfortable, consider your buying options.

3. There are no bad skis.

Every ski on the rack is built to suit a certain ability and, in some cases, a different condition and skiing style. The only real danger in the marketplace is a salesperson who sells the wrong equipment to the consumer. Make sure you buy equipment that suits your needs and ability.

4. Take your time buying ski boots.

Ski boots today are built to perform and fit comfortably. Everybody's feet are different; some boots won't fit you. Spend a lot of time walking around in the boots. Never buy a boot on the first day out shopping. Try as many different pairs as possible and try them on several different times. Remember, boots are more flexible at room temperature; they will stiffen up in the cold.

5. Bindings are based on weight only.

Don't fall for the bells and whistles on bindings. They all perform according to weight, plain and simple. The most important thing is to have your old bindings checked at the start of every season, or buy new ones according to your weight and ability. To keep bindings in working order, cover them when skis are on top of a car to keep them free from sand, dirt, and salt. Plus, make sure that your boot soles are in good shape and not too worn. Boots are an important aspect of bindings releasing properly.

Ski Tuning Gives the Performance Edge

Taking good care of your ski equipment will help make you a better, safer skier and will enhance your enjoyment of skiing. One thing skiers often overlook is the fact that a proper ski tuning can give them the performance edge – pun intended! But a sharp edge is not all there is to a ski-tune. I've met many skiers who only have their skis sharpened and hot-waxed at the beginning of each season. They do a disservice to both their skis and their skiing by not maintaining a sharp edge and a good ski surface.

Most ski shops can give you a new edge and a hot wax in about ten minutes. They'll remove the burrs from the edges and smooth the surface on the sanding belt, but a real tune-up takes about 45 minutes and can't be done solely on a sanding machine. It takes not only a machine but some hand tools as well to properly tune a ski.

A proper ski tune-up begins with removing the old wax with a solvent. A sanding machine is used to remove burrs from the edges. Then the ski base is examined for gouges and nicks which are repaired with P-tex, a plastic heated in a glue gun and applied to the base. Using a plane with a special carbide blade, the excess plastic is removed.

Next, a stone grinding wheel is used to level the edges with the base. When you're skiing, if the edges touch before the base, you get rail skis with no control. If the base touches before the edges, you get what's called "base high" and you can't get an edge. The only way to get a perfectly flat base is with a stonegrind.

Attention now turns to the edges. Special chromium files with a more pronounced cutting angle than a hardware store bastard file are used to hand-file the edges and base. These files also make it easier to vary the bevel, or edge sharpness, from tip to center to tail. You don't want the ski tips sharpened, as they're not needed for control. The job is finished with a 4-inch long diamond sharpening tool. Many skiers carry one of these in their pocket so that they can quickly resharpen their edges while they're on the slopes. Then a polystone, a type of rubber abrasive, is used to deburr and polish the edges. Now the edges are smooth as glass and keenly sharp.

The handwork is now finished and it's time to run the skis across the stone once again. The stone grinder puts a pattern on the ski base, tiny microgrooves that form a structure to give the ski more control. If no sparks fly during this stonegrind, the base and edges are perfectly level.

The final phase is hot waxing. The base is very porous, and it will accept a lot of wax. The hot wax pours in to fill those pores. That's why there is no substitute for hot waxing. Every racer waxes his or her skis this way. With the wax applied and cooled, the excess is scraped away with a plastic tool to make sure that there is no wax on the edges. With that done, the finishing touch is running a fine brass wire brush up and down the ski. Now the microgroove pattern emerges and is very much in evidence. These skis are ready to take to the slopes.

For the average skier, skis should probably be tuned after every five or six trips to the slopes. Man-made snow dulls skis more quickly than natural snow. It's denser, harder snow, and it takes the edge off more quickly. But the proof of the ski tuning is in powder. The difference is so noticeable that you'll feel as if you were on new skis.

About the Photographer

Born in Pennsylvania, Dennis Welsh has been a freelance photographer in Maine since 1990, specializing in outdoor adventure sports. A frequent contributor *to Snow Country Magazine, Ski*, and *Skier Magazine*, Welsh's work has also appeared in *Runner's World, Tennis, Sports Illustrated*, and *Warren Miller's Ski World*. His stock library is represented by Adventure Photo & Film in Ventura, California. He and his wife, Anne Ball, currently live in Yarmouth, Maine.

About the Authors

Dan Egan's Story

Growing up in Milton, Massachusetts, only minutes from the Blue Hill Ski area, Dan Egan was shredding by the age of five. Today, he challenges the most extreme terrain in the world, skiing the unskiable in Turkey, Romania, Russia, Mongolia, Chile, and Yugoslavia for the U.S. Extreme Team, Warren Miller, and his own film productions.

During high school, Dan skied every chance he got, but placed his professional ski career on hold while pursuing a college education. Dan attended Babson College where he studied Business Finance and Marketing and competed for the ski team. He first filmed for Warren Miller in 1985 while still in college.

In 1987, with diploma in hand, Dan packed his bags and moved to Squaw Valley, California, home base of U.S. extreme skiers. The still-emerging daredevil sport of extreme skiing became Dan's hobby, passion, and eventually his career. Dan was quickly noticed by this elite group of skiers, film makers, and sponsors and has since become one of the greatest extreme skiers in history.

Competing on the World Pro Mogul Tour from 1988 through 1989 and ranked among the top 16 in the world, Dan's reputation preceded him. Great film makers such as Warren Miller and Eric Perlman could not get enough of Dan and his older brother John for their movies and videos.

Warren Miller has been an International Award-Winning sports film producer for over 45 years and has used Dan in 12 of his films. Eric Perlman produced "The North Face Extreme Skiing Video

Series," six in all, which starred the North Face Extreme Team, of which Dan was a member.

Dan has become an award-winning producer in his own right. His films include "World Wide and Wild," which won third place at the 1989 International Ski Film Festival; "Decade of Descents" in 1990; "The Raging Russian, Disaster on Mt. Elbrus," winner of a Telly Award in 1990, "The Extreme Dream," called the best film of 1992 by *Skiing* Magazine; "Return of the Shred-I," which took third place in the 1993 International Ski Film Festival; and "Children of the Snow," winner of the 1995 International Ski Film Festival.

With one dream accomplished and others on the horizon, Dan is devoted to creating informational and educational tools and resources, i.e., videos and books for children and other amateur ski enthusiasts. Dan also cultivates marketing opportunities for companies such as GMC, Mountain Dew, Coors, Dynastar, and Fila. A new production is "Where the Steeps Have No Name," sponsored by Miller Brewing Company.

The Egan Entertainment Network, Inc. (EEN) was founded by Dan Egan in 1989 to market and promote skiing around the world. Through grassroots marketing efforts, Egan has created promotions and multimedia shows reaching consumers at theaters, ski shows, retailers, corporations, and universities around the world.

Dan has become a role model for extreme skiers and an educator and effective motivational speaker. He is currently a member of the U.S. Extreme Team and the Executive Director of SKI 93, a consortium of ski areas situated on Route 93 in New Hampshire's White Mountains.

Mihaela Fera's Story

Mihaela "Miki" Fera's story begins in a small village near the town of Sibiu in Romania where her grandmother, dying on a battlefield, gave birth to Mihaela's mother in 1944. Adopted by a Romanian Colonel's wife, her mother grew up in Bistrita in Moldavia. She graduated from the University in Cluj and became a school teacher in Sibiu where she met Mihaela's father, also a teacher.

Born on August 6, 1970, Mihaela grew up in Communist Romania. "They were difficult times," recounts Mihaela. "It was very hard on my family. My father even left Romania for three years to find work. The one thing that kept my family together was a common love for athletics."

Mihaela remembers: "It was understood that my sister and I would follow in my parents' footsteps. They taught us the importance and necessity of a healthy body. They would tell us 'Mens sana in corpore sano' or 'What your mind desires, the body has to fulfill.'"

Skiing eventually became her passion. "The snow, with its wonders and its beauty, drew me to the sport," Mihaela states. Starting when she was nine, it took Mihaela only four years to qualify for the Romanian National ski team, and she was just 14 when she won her first Gold Medal at the Senior National Championships in 1984.

Mihaela competed in the European Junior Championships in 1985 and made a strong third-place finish. The two women who beat her went on to be ranked Number 1 and Number 2 in the world in 1992. They were Austrian Eder Elferied and Pernilla Wiberg of Sweden, who was the World Champion in 1991 and the 1994 Gold Medal winner. Unfortunately, Mihaela was forced to return and train behind the Iron Curtain with inadequate training conditions and very little funding.

"I had to constantly remind myself why I was skiing," Mihaela says. In 1988, at the age of 18, she participated in her first Olympic Games in Calgary, Alberta, Canada, where she finished 21st in the Downhill event. "It was at the point, however, that I realized that with my lack of support in Romania, the two girls who had beat me at the Junior Championships in '85 were pulling further and further away."

In 1989 the Communist government collapsed in Romania and funding for state-sponsored sports programs dried up. "Things were so bad in 1993 that I strained with sticks for racing gates." Miki continued to compete internationally and, in 1992, she placed in the top 25 in every Alpine event at the Olympics in Alberteville and, in 1994, she placed 20th in the Combined event at the Olympics in Lillehammer.

Life changed when she met her husband, extreme skier Dan Egan, who was on a film shoot in Transylvania. After the Lillehammer Olympics, they were married. "My ski career has had a second life," states Mihaela. "In this country I have been able to pursue my passion and it has paid off."

Competing on a level playing field, she has regained her status as one of the best women ski racers in the world. In 1994-95 she competed in the World Cup Races here in the United States and on the NORM circuit. In 1996 she competed on the Whenever Women's World Pro Ski Tour and won "Rookie of the Year," finishing in the top four in every Grand Slalom race but two.

In 1996-97, Mihaela plans to compete once again on the World Cup and NORM circuits to keep her FIS

(Federation of International Skiing) points in order to qualify for the 1998 Romanian Olympic Team. She will also compete on the Women's World Pro Ski Tour.

Mihaela is the international spokesperson for Nobody's Children, a non-profit organization dedicated to helping doctors treat children in economic and war-torn countries throughout the world, like Romania and Bosnia. "I was very fortunate to travel during the Communist era," Miki comments. "I want to give back to the less fortunate by helping to shed some light on the tragedies that are taking place with orphaned children in Eastern Europe."

Nobody's Children

Nobody's Children was established to provide medical and humanitarian resources for needy children throughout the world.

Nobody's Children was founded by Ed and Elaine Yourtee after their 1991 experiences in Romania while adopting their son Jonathan. Initial efforts were directed toward helping the children of Romania. Last year, we were able to begin working with refugee children in Bosnia as well, and now we operate as a registered NGO in Bosnia with UN clearances.

Our principal sources of support have been local fundraising events, responses to our newsletters, donations from churches and community organizations, donations from travelers who have visited the camp in Bosnia, grants from a small private foundation, and sale of logo items. Nobody's Children is an IRS approved tax-exempt 501(c)(3)(a) organization. All our projects are accomplished with no paid staff. Ninety-five percent of all contributions go directly toward program and related expenses.

Official spokesperson: Mihaela Fera Egan, three-time Romanian Olympic downhill skiier

Nobody's Children
P.O. Box 1076
Windham, New Hampshire 03087-1076
Phone/Fax 603. 893.0925

E-mail:ELY@yrte.mv.com
Web Page: http:///www.mv.com/ipusers/yrte

Outrageous Action-Packed Ski Videos!

featuring world-renowned extreme skiers Dan & John Egan

The Extreme Dream, subtitled "A Motivational Ski Documentary," is John and Dan's first video. It includes original footage as well as clips from previous appearances with Warren Miller. The video emphasizes "living in the direction of your dreams," taken from Joseph Campbell's work on myth and the notion of following your bliss, The Egans touch on the somber side of the quest for the extreme when a fellow adventurer dies during a sudden snowstorm. Says Dan, "What matters most is not a nice car and house, but having love, passion and desire."

60 minutes. $14.95

Return of the Shred-I, The Egan brothers and the DesLauriers trek through Romania, Lebanon, Russia, British Columbia and the U.S. for dramatic footage of top athletes who attempt to master snowboarding, telemarking, Alpine skiing, and windsurfing. Find out who can do it all.

48 minutes. $19.95

Children of the Snow, Winner of the 1995 International Ski Film Festival, Dan Egan created this video to educate and motivate children in skiing, snowboarding and outdoor winter activities in the mountains. Covers everything from safety to geography to bloopers. Fast-paced and very entertaining.

30 minutes. $14.95

To Order call

1-800-619-6801